MW00619085

MAGNIFICENT GENERATION

MILLENNIALS
or it could be Xers or Zers, but it's
probably too late for Boomers

James Nelson
with
Matt Thornton

Published by
MagGen Group, LLC

To Scott

Perhaps one measure of a man is how badly he is missed after all these years.

CONTENTS

INTRODUCTION

Not long ago, an acquaintance of mine told me a Millennial joke. I do not remember what the specifics were, but when he finished, I casually asked him if he thought Seal Team Six had ever accepted Millennials as part of the team. Upon reflection, he acknowledged there was probably a substantial number. He had not thought about that. I could have just as readily asked him if he thought there were very many Millennials who had served in any of the branches of our Armed Forces fighting brutal wars or in the medical profession or any of the exacting jobs throughout our nation. Of course, the answer to all of these is an emphatic yes. I was not trying to make my friend uncomfortable. I was honestly trying to draw attention to the problem of judging an entire generation by looking at a few select groups.

I also find it interesting when someone older categorically criticizes a younger generation when that older generation is, to a certain extent, the ones who are responsible for how they turned out. The older generation is the one who has either raised, taught, or trained these kids, and now they are criticizing the outcome. Since this paradox is not exactly lost on the young, do you think there might be just a little push back? No wonder we have expressions like "OK, Boomer." Previous generations would have pushed back as well, only probably with more forceful language.

We should also ask ourselves, would previous generations have responded differently to the onslaught of social media that has come upon us in the last 20 years. Tech giants have, for the most part, experimented on Millennials. Almost everything that can be used for good can also be used for bad, and it takes a while to sort these things out.

Throughout history, the old have probably always goaded the young. Younger people likely have always pushed back. Although some of this is normal, I think it goes beyond normal in our present situation because of the prevailing cultural divide. I am pointing these things out so we can perhaps step back a little and have some perspective. One of the goals of that perspective is to objectively consider what might even define a great generation. More than likely, we will only perceive greatness decades from now; but in that greatness, we will see that there was a battle and a victory overcoming false and destructive ideas with the true and the good. The Millennial generation is uniquely positioned to fight just that kind of battle. We have a cultural divide fiercely dividing our nation, and they are getting to the age where they will soon exert considerable influence.

A consistent premise in this book is that when people live through a time where they believe painfully destructive falsehoods, and then learn the truth, they become powerful advocates for that truth. They may even pass it on to future generations. A simple example of this premise is when people go along with the idea that massive debt is no problem. When they find that owing others vast amounts of money is like being imprisoned, since one is not free to do the things you would like to do, they have their eyes opened. Once they fight their way out of the dark hole of debt, these are the ones who pass on to everyone they know just how bad debt is.

Another example is when a nation estimates a potential enemy's intentions and not their actual capabilities. Their lack of vigilance and preparation then leads to a long and costly war.

That actually happened in the lead up to World War II when England's leadership believed Germany's intentions were benign. When you learn life's difficult lessons the hard way, it changes you.

In this book we will examine several areas and situations where people have learned some things the hard way, through tough consequences and deep, hard thought. Many of the areas discussed may be very new to you because they are not part of the prevailing public discourse today. And you, the reader, can determine if they are true and relevant to your life. They may be life-changing and even nation-changing.

At this point, you might ask what qualifies a person to write a book directed to younger generations concerning their potential. My work requires me to travel extensively, nationally and internationally, and many of my coworkers are Millennials. In the last several years, I have conducted a syntopical reading of over 160 books on various subjects.[1] Two of the three children my wife and I have raised are Millennials. I have taught Gen Xers and Millennials in a volunteer capacity for more than 20 years and worked with them on various volunteer projects. No single person, though, has all the credentials to cover such a broad topic. My experience does give some much needed real-world perspective gained over three decades.

One person who is qualified is my friend and contributor to this book, Matt Thornton. His age and trials put him right in the heart of the Millennial generation. As a talented two-sport athlete in high school, he saw the best of teenage life and, at the same time, its deepest lows as he mourned the loss of his father, my best friend. He is an outdoorsy guy who graduated from a private college in the southeast United States but also attended NYU while modeling with the Ford modeling agency. He has worked at a prestigious hi-tech company in Silicon Valley, and then not long after, found himself virtually homeless in Los Angeles, chasing his entrepreneurial dreams. Social media has been his close companion through it all.

Matt and I are very close friends, and yet we do not agree on everything. Over the years of our relationship, we have had a few significant disagreements, yet our friendship has never wavered. One thing we have found is that tolerance requires disagreement, or there isn't anything to tolerate. Disagreement is OK, and every person is free to form their own opinion within the forum of private and public debate. We find that we often learn a great deal from people who do not necessarily agree with us.

We also acknowledge that we carry a certain amount of bias. I probably carry some bias from the fact that I like young people, or I would not have volunteered my time teaching, mentoring, or working with them over the last 30 years. Matt's bias comes from the fact that he is a Millennial. However, every person on the planet carries some bias since we are not machines; and yet, we can still observe and speak the truth. The famous historical example of this is Holocaust survivors. Although they were most certainly biased, the survivors nevertheless vociferously spoke the truth so that what happened to them would not happen to anybody else.

President Obama, in late October 2019, made a particularly insightful statement. *The Washington Post* reported:

Former President Barack Obama offered some advice earlier this week to young people hoping to change society: participating in cancel culture isn't the way to do it. "This idea of purity and you're never compromised and you're always politically woke and all that stuff, you should get over that quickly," the 58-year-old said Tuesday while speaking at the Obama Foundation Summit in Chicago. "The world is messy. There are ambiguities. People who do really good stuff have flaws."[2]

All people everywhere are flawed. If we were to discard every idea in history because the people they originated from were not perfect, we would learn nothing. Matt and I are also flawed. This book will examine a lot of situations, and it may appear that we are judging people who thought certain things or who made mistakes, but often these people are ourselves. We are not judging people but ideas. We firmly believe people are equal, but ideas are not. Bad ideas have bad consequences, and good ideas have good consequences. Ideas lead to actions, so you might also say that we are not judging people but their actions and trying to learn something in the process.

Millennials, in general, I have found are asking great questions. Investigating life's most important questions is a fantastic endeavor, and all significant undertakings require effort. A few areas in the book may require more effort than others. Some readers may even want to put specific ideas up on a mental shelf to ponder and return to them later.

Matt is the reason this work came into being. He is the one who asked the probing questions that started the discussion.

1

SUCCESS

Could Someone Please
Tell Me What It Is?

OH GREAT, ANOTHER BRAG TAG. Why do you even click on it? The so-called friend is not really close, but for some reason, they are the type of person you subconsciously compare yourself to. When you finally finish checking it all out, there is an empty feeling you cannot quite shake. All the facebragging, disguised or otherwise, seems to leave an overall sense of inadequacy–that you are not successful. An ambiguous and fleeting interpretation of success causes much angst, frustration, and even depression today as people try to figure out their world.

The definition of success is the achievement of something desired, planned, or attempted.[1] When used in reference to someone's overall life, many cultures infer an element of fame or fortune. One problem with the fame and fortune part is that many people in history have had fame or fortune or both and were thoroughly evil. Another interesting phenomenon is that people can have fame and fortune and not be happy. You have to look no further than Hollywood to see this. It seems fairly common that people strive and strive, just knowing total fulfillment is theirs when they achieve their ultimate goal. When they do reach the goal, they find that it did not totally fulfill them, and they are devastated.

Now, I am going to add one more disheartening dimension to this idea of success. If and when you think you might have it figured out, social media will more than likely change the target. Just when you settle on a satisfying interpretation of success, the herd changes the definition. Is it possible we should maybe extract our vision of success from something a little more durable? Is it really success if you are miserable during and after the quest? What in the world makes us happy, anyway?

NEEDS

We all have some definite needs. It is obvious we have four physiological needs: air, water, food, and covering or shelter. Nobody disputes this. We all also have some very real psychological needs, and no one seems to talk about this at the gym or on television. Psychologists tend to organize these or label these needs somewhat differently, but the following definitions work well for most people in the real world.[2]

The first one is love and acceptance.[3] We usually derive love and acceptance from close family and personal relationships, and women typically excel here far more than men. Men need relationships, but for some reason do not seem to prioritize them much of the time. Women, on the other hand, are built for good, close family and friends. When this is not happening, men may be badly bothered, but women are devastated.

The second psychological need is feelings of competence.[4] We all have skills, and we need an outlet to develop them and use them. People may think they would achieve lasting happiness if they could just retire and do nothing, but usually find out they are quickly bored. You can only golf, travel, or fish for so long. We can derive feelings of competence from hobbies and volunteerism, but a primary driver of this for most people is work. That work can be at a job or raising children or both—but we all seem to need meaningful work.

The third psychological need is praise and recognition leading to feelings of worthiness.[5] Praise and recognition come from our interactions with other people. Again, volunteerism and hobbies can provide that interaction as well as relationships with family and friends. However, work is still a primary source for meeting this need. Unfortunately, for whatever reason, there are many managers out there who are quite sparse in their words of encouragement, so praise and recognition frequently come in the form of a paycheck. At least you know you earned it, and that is key here because feelings of worthiness come from praise and recognition that you know are earned. We are hardwired to earn.

Business owners and managers should note that need numbers two and three are tremendously important for you to know. Feelings of competence are derived much better when an employee is properly trained and knows what is expected of them. Properly given praise and recognition, leading to feelings of worthiness, is very powerful and motivates people beyond what you might ever imagine. Additionally, parents and teachers need to know this regarding the raising and teaching of children.

The fourth and last primary psychological need is purpose.[6] Purpose has to do with the reason why, as in, "Why am I getting up to go to work, or take care of kids, or whatever, on a crummy Monday in January?" The reason may very well be that those we love, with whom we are in a very close relationship, depend upon us. Another reason may be that we also would like to have some financial resources that give us some control and freedom in our life. These are all excellent reasons for getting up and going to work, but what if you were rich beyond belief?

ROCKEFELLER

John D. Rockefeller had tons of money and didn't need to get up. John Davison Rockefeller (1839 – 1937) was born into modest circumstances in upstate New York. His first job was as an assistant bookkeeper for a small produce commission firm in Cleveland. He learned a great deal about transportation costs and the shipping of goods and started his own business at age 20 with a partner. The produce commission business did exceptionally well during the Civil War. At the perfect time, as the war was winding down, the partners decided to start an oil refinery as the oil industry began to boom. Kerosene had become the most economical form of lighting oil, and demand was skyrocketing.

Rockefeller was an astute businessman—some would say ruthless. He bought out his partners and then started buying out the competition. Many of the methods he used to crush his rivals are illegal today. However, at that time, most of his business practices were still legal. He started Standard Oil and grew it to the point of controlling 90% of the market. He was remarkably frugal and never wasted anything. There was an exceptionally noxious and flammable byproduct (now known as gasoline) from the refining of kerosene. People would just dump it in the rivers at night or anywhere else they could covertly unload it. Several rivers even caught on fire when sparks from riverboats and other sources hit a river contaminated with gasoline waste.

Rockefeller was so thrifty he wanted to use the gasoline for something. He decided to use it as a fuel to run his refineries and went on to find other applications for it as well:

Before the automobile, nobody knew what to do with the light fraction of crude oil known as gasoline, and many refiners, under cover of dark, let this waste product run into the river "we used to burn it for fuel in distilling the oil," said Rockefeller, "and thousands and hundreds of thousands of barrels of it floated down the creeks and rivers, and the ground was saturated with it, in the constant effort to get rid of it."[7]

It is astonishing for us in our present time to think that no one knew what to do with gasoline. Rockefeller's thriftiness, not wanting to waste a thing, reduced pollution and positioned him unbelievably well for the future. When kerosene's price began to fall, Standard Oil had already configured itself to produce large amounts of gasoline for automobiles.

By the time Rockefeller was in his 50s, his health had started to deteriorate, and he suffered from depression. At about this time, he retired from day-to-day operations of the oil business and devoted his time almost exclusively to giving more of his money away. Rockefeller's peak net worth was estimated at up to $900 million (about $280 billion in today's dollars), and he gave away during his lifetime about $540 million (close to $170 billion in today's dollars). He gave to the poor, universities, medical and scientific research, and many other causes. In the last 30 years of his life, he was found to be much more content and finally passed away at age 97. Rockefeller discovered great purpose in life helping others and went from one of the most ruthless and disliked businessmen in the world to one of the world's most generous philanthropists.

Helping others gives us great purpose and is another excellent reason for getting up in the morning. We all need a purpose in our life to have meaning in what we do. The first three needs pointed to the importance of relationships and work, and they also reinforced purpose. Taking care of family and going to work both exude purpose. In that respect, these needs are very interrelated.

This is all well and good, but you may still ask, what again do these needs have to do with success? Well, here is the reality. Suppose you are chasing after the world's view, social media's view, or someone else's view of success that ignores these primary psychological needs. In that case, you are chasing the wind and likely to end up depressed or miserable in the process. We need to remember these needs. Years ago, I developed a kind of a weird acronym to help me remember them: the L and A stand for Love and Acceptance, and the C stands for feelings of Competence. The saying simply states that things will not go well if you LAC (lack) Praise (and recognition leading to feelings of worthiness) and Purpose. Yeah, it might be a little weird, but I've never forgotten it. There are some things you do not want to forget—ever.

RELATIONSHIPS AND WORK

In discussing these psychological needs, something that stands out is how important both relationships and work are to their fulfillment. Is it possible that someone who has a couple of good family relationships or a couple of good, close friends and a job are well on their way to success and do not know it? I would go so far as to say that if you have one good close relationship and are studying or striving to get a job, you are very close to achieving success.

You may not be buying this, so let's look at a couple of situations and see how this plays out. You might still want to cling to the fame and fortune idea; but we already know people who sacrificed everything, including their relationships, striving for fame and fortune. They finally achieve that "huge breakthrough" and find it kind of hollow. They develop other relationships and wonder if people only value them for their fame or fortune. The rest of us do not consume ourselves with this type of worry. You discover great contentment when you find people who like you or love you for who you are.

Another example is when someone inherits a considerable sum of money or (even though the odds are extremely low) wins the lottery. What is the first thing a person does with their new found wealth? They quit work. Is it any wonder that later they are adrift in life and not very happy. They may have discarded the very source of their feelings of competency and earned praise, not to mention purpose.

For several years I volunteered as a mentor for kids within the Department of Juvenile Justice in South Metro Atlanta. The teenagers I mentored would often ask questions about work and good and bad jobs. I would always tell them the only bad job is no job. You learn something from every job, even if it is the fact that you might not want to do that particular work for the rest of your life. In a job, you usually interact with other people and, therefore make contacts, which can help in finding something better if so desired. Here is the real catch, though. You are never more wanted than when you are already employed, developing a work history that shows you know how to show up for work on time and interact with others. One of the kids I mentored stayed in his job a little over a year and then decided he wanted to apply for a different one. He came back and told me he could not believe how many jobs there were and how many businesses wanted to hire him. I am convinced employers wanted him to work for them because he stayed in his previous position for over a year and always showed up on time. While employed, he developed self-confidence from competence gained in the workplace. Another end benefit for him were feelings of worthiness derived from so many employers wanting to hire him.

Another advantage of work is the opportunity to develop relationships with coworkers. Again, this happens quite naturally with women, but men also quickly develop relationships at work. It seems very natural for men to grow close to others when working shoulder to shoulder with them doing tough stuff and overcoming obstacles together. In my own life, I think some of my most fun moments were doing things with the guys I work with like playing in an indoor soccer league, softball, or flag football and then all going out together somewhere afterward to hang out and banter with one another. We somehow forget how fantastic these moments are.

The discussion on work so far has focused a great deal on employment outside the home. We need to ensure we do not overlook another critical job by asking a rare question. What is the most important task of a civilization? The most important task of a civilization is the upbringing of its children. A person almost has to wonder why the question is either not asked or not answered in this way. At any rate, many people tend to think the major task of a civilization is developing technology, military preparedness, infrastructure, or something else—but there should be no debate about this. The very word "civilization" implies a culture lasting an extended length of time. The people who will bring about our future technology, national defense, infrastructure, and businesses are today's children. If you work teaching or are involved in raising children, you are entrusted with a vitally important job, valuable beyond belief. We need to direct the nation's esteem and resources accordingly. If we do not do well here, we are toast in the future.

BUT IS SOMETHING STILL MISSING?

As stated before, if you have a good relationship with someone or others and are involved in real work or the studying and preparation for future work, you are well on the way to success. There might still be something missing, though. That something is the ideal of treating others the way you would like to be treated. You cannot do this very well, however, until you know how worthwhile you are already as someone who pursues good relationships and good, healthy work that serves others. This is because there is a subtle and elusive dilemma lurking below the surface. The dilemma is: you cannot treat others well, as you would like to be treated yourself, if you have a poor self-image of your worth. People who are overly disappointed with themselves or just down on themselves tend to draw inward. Even though they do not desire to, they tend to focus excessively on themselves. This downward cycle can make you half crazy. I encourage you to speak against the voices from inside or outside that say, "You will never amount to anything...that was so stupid...you will never be good enough." These words are not the final truth about you, and these thoughts need to be taken captive. You may need to state aloud, "That is not who I am," and end it.

This whole notion about treating others the way you would like to be treated is no small thing. We simply do not realize how many behaviors are kept in check by this idea. When this concept pervades a society do expect less conflict, meanness, corruption, and other various crimes. However, we are all flawed, imperfect people, and so no society will achieve perfection. We obviously need—and will need—good and sensible laws.

PUTTING IT ALL TOGETHER

We can now finally look at the whole picture. There truly was something missing because there are many so-called successful people whose behavior we do not want to emulate. Part of achieving success is treating others well, and we must have some guidelines to do so. One of the best guidelines ever used is serving or treating others how we like to be treated. When you combine this with developing good relationships and working at, or towards, an occupation that provides a paycheck or helps others, then you are a success and also have great purpose in your life. Please note that this definition does not encourage you to focus too much on your achievements so as to make your world a movie about yourself. Instead, a person humbly knows they are pursuing the right things, which frees them up to think of others more.

At this point, someone might think that this definition of success does not account for ambition or improving ourselves. This is simply not true. We all need to set goals to improve our life or circumstances. This is another one of life's great purposes. The main point I am making, though, is that there is great success leading up to and during the quest to improve your life. Every person should strive to find the occupation or profession that truly makes them come alive. The only way to do that is to enter the arena and find out what you like to do and what talents you bring to the table. Frequently, the things you are good at are also the things you like to do, but we will not find out unless we try some different jobs and possibly invest in some preparation.

We are all made for creative work. Nevertheless, we often have to work at non-creative things until we have the financial freedom or training to pursue work that excites us. Musicians and other artists have an advantage here because their work is creative from the start. Unfortunately, with the emergence of national and global media and massive urbanization, only a select few can earn a good living through the arts. In a perfect world, more artists could support themselves well while connected to smaller or medium-sized communities. In the meantime, some passions are destined to be hobbies or second jobs. No matter what our creative pursuit is, we should always be seeking to improve ourselves. We do all this with the realization that our final success is not dependent upon reaching some ultimate goal, but that there is great success and growth in the process.

We also should acknowledge that success is often not measured in the exact level of the achievement, but in what is overcome. I did volunteer work with a man who grew up fatherless in a drug-infested neighborhood in Virginia, and at age 18 he was incarcerated for selling drugs. Irving had the equivalent of about a sixth-grade education. When I worked alongside him, he was out of prison and working on his master's degree. I cannot begin to tell you what an incredible success I thought he was even though he had neither fame nor fortune. We all have different circumstances to overcome. None of us starts from the same initial conditions in life. Based on what you have overcome, you may be "hitting it out of the park" and not even know it.

Fame and fortune are not necessarily bad in and of themselves. Meritorious service to others can sometimes bring fame. Worthy causes are also frequently supported or bolstered by famous people. Wealth is often the natural outcome for people when they find what they truly love to do, are good at it, and work diligently. Wealth also accomplishes great purposes when people invest in businesses that employ people or give it to those in need. Even when people use their wealth to buy things they like, they are employing others who make the product. We should remember that real wealth is probably best defined by the things that we have that are worth far more than money.[8] Family and close relationships are what immediately come to mind.

Perhaps a good test to see if this characterization of success rings true is to see the opposite application. What do you think of a person who neglects their family and other relationships, hates any kind of work, and treats others poorly? These attributes are probably as opposite the definition of success as is possible. An interesting correlating side note occurs at the neighborhood level. If you have community leadership that does not fiercely fight for strong families and the institutions that support them, sound education leading to work, and treating others well, then perhaps your leaders are committed to other things besides your well-being.

A well-grounded, functional definition of success is incredibly important for individuals, communities, and leaders to comprehend. Everyone suffers when we waste too much of our time and energy chasing misguided ambitions. When we are aware of the dimensions of life that truly matter, we can transcend the trivial as we lay a firm foundation for the future.

You may still disagree with the definition of success expounded upon in this chapter because maybe you think it aims too low, or it's not exactly what you have in mind, and that is fine. I only ask that you look at the world around you and consider that most of the good and beautiful you see exist because people, past or present, highly valued family and relationships, work, and treating others the way they would like to be treated themselves.

2

RELATIONSHIPS
Floating Down the River

IT IS SOMEWHAT COMMON NOW for men and women, after progressing out of the dating phase, to move in together. In fact, this has become more and more common over the last 40 years to the extent that you could almost call it old-fashioned at this point. I liken this arrangement to a man and a woman deciding to live together in a boat floating down a river. We will call the river The River of You Can Do Anything You Want and There Are No Consequences. The arrangement looks like it is going to be a huge blast for everyone involved. As you start your journey on the river, everything is usually quite fun, and the ride reasonably smooth as you float along exploring the different bends and terrain. After a while, though, you seem to run into more crosscurrents and even a little white water. Finally, after a notoriously rough encounter, one of the occupants notices someone else on the bank. They appear quite attractive. As the boat swerves and turns near the shore, he jumps out to the bank right next to this new person. As you float off, you look back and notice they are walking off hand in hand, and he waves to you. This feels kind of cruel.

When he pushed off, you also noticed he inadvertently pushed the boat out into the middle of the river into faster water. Just about then, you feel, and then you actually hear the low roar in the distance. The further along you go, the more intense it gets until you find yourself plunging over a hundred-foot waterfall. The boat splinters apart, and you are about half-drowned as you pull yourself to shore. It feels like your arm is nearly pulled out from the rib cage with your heart wholly exposed. As you collect your thoughts, it occurs to you the only way this could have been worse is if there was a child aboard. At about that time, someone a little younger than you appears on the bank and exclaims, "Isn't this river a blast!"

Many are finding that the breakup from these relationships feels every bit as bad as a divorce, and several divorces can scar the human heart. I did not necessarily mean to pick on men in the previous situation since either one can eventually decide to jump out of the boat. However, I think men definitely have the best temporary arrangement when they enter and exit live-together relationships. One sincere young woman admitted that she felt like she was endlessly auditioning to be his wife, and it was getting really old. It reminds me of what Harvey Weinstein did; only the casting couch was probably more short-term.

MARRIAGE

Now what we may hear from men at this point is, "I don't need a piece of paper to say I love you." Binding promises have been an expression of love for thousands of years of written history.[1] There is no greater binding promise than when a man stands up in front of family and friends and promises to love this woman for the rest of his life, in sickness and in health. Let's be clear, when a man says he does not need a piece of paper to say he loves you, what he is really saying is that he does not love you enough to stand up in front of the community and commit his love until "death do us part."[2]

Right now you are probably thinking that I am really being hard on men. That is somewhat true, but I also am pointing these things out because I also am a man, have done some of these things myself, and know the incredible temptations involved. I also know most men actually want to do the right thing. There is something deep within us that wants to do the honorable. Having high expectations of the younger generation is a compliment and shows that we have confidence in them. There is something damaging that occurs when we treat people like they cannot handle the tough things in life. It is like when parents still hover over their older children or mow down every obstacle in their path. You are telling them by your actions that you do not think they can make it on their own.

Boomers now in their 60s or 70s are the ones who fled to Canada, or advocated doing so, during the unpopular Vietnam War. The mantra of the time was "if-it-feels-good-do-it." Frequently, the same went for marriages. If you were not happy in your marriage, then "just get a divorce." Many of these same people became the prime influencers in media and our universities, and they have had a significant impact on our culture. If we look around at the state of the family today, can we really say that we are better off for it? Do you want to be like them? I honestly think you are better than that.

Men often do want to be honorable in their relationships, but they definitely need some help. Women are probably the ones who are more apt to want to keep dating fun and not get sexually involved during this phase. Dating should be fun. This is the time you get to do a lot of great activities together, and hopefully, spend time with friends and family so they can check out the new person in your life. It is remarkable how conflicted everything gets, though, when it goes beyond the fun dating phase. Many young couples probably believe that if they live together first, they will know one another better and, therefore, have less chance of a divorce. However, the data simply does not back this up. Long term research still shows cohabiting before marriage increases your chance of a divorce.[3] The Pew Research Center also notes married adults are more likely than those living with a partner to say things are going very well in their relationship (58% vs. 41%).[4]

It is kind of interesting to think about, but if all women decided that dating would only be dating and there was not going to be a sexual relationship until after the wedding ceremony, every wedding venue in the country would immediately be booked into the distant future. Women hear or feel many different messages concerning their worth, but the truest message they should hear is summed up in For King and Country's song *Priceless*. For most men, a wife is simply priceless.

KEEPING IT TOGETHER

In marriages today, though, we undoubtedly have a bad case of "you can't live without them, and you can't live with them." Today's divorce rate is somewhere between 40% and 50%, and though it has somewhat decreased in the last decade, it is still higher than anyone would like.[5] After 50 years of the divorce numbers getting out of control, I think we now know some truths that can give a marriage a better chance.

Falling in love and getting married is one of life's greatest experiences. The only problem with the falling in love part is that you can also fall out of love quite easily. There are days when I'm just not feeling it—and the same goes for my wife. Emotions naturally ebb and flow, so is it possible we need a better definition for long-lasting marital love? A definition anchored in something beyond ourselves that doesn't collapse under the weight of our expectations. Many think a better definition of this kind of love is the willing self-sacrifice for the good of another without them having earned it or having to pay you back. This is precisely the kind of love we are not naturally good at giving. This has to be lived out and requires us to grow—and when I say grow, I mean primarily grow less selfish. People who move on from relationship to relationship are usually never required to grow much in this way. The romantic feelings of love are very real and wonderful, but they must be paired with sacrificial love to endure.

We all enter marriage thinking it is going to be easier than it really is. Many of life's pursuits are difficult, and we still end up enjoying them a great deal. Someone does not become an exceptional ballet dancer strictly because it was easy for them, and the same goes for professional athletes. They dedicate themselves to their dance or their sport, knowing they have to work at it. Marriage is no different. Perhaps we can even compare marriage somewhat to skiing or snowboarding. It is a lot of fun when you start out, but eventually, you find yourself in a mogul field, a long line of bumps, and you are not quite ready for the challenge. After getting bounced around, you finally navigate out of them onto some smooth terrain. If you practice and do not give up though, you eventually get to the point where you can ski or snowboard through any kind of terrain, which gives you a great feeling. You also will need some vision—you will not navigate the bumps well when blinded by heavy snow, glare, or if you are just not paying attention.

Some of the most sizable bumps in marriage are tight finances, young children, and teenagers. If you are in the phase of life where you have toddlers and a dismal sized checking account, please know this is a challenging time and that you are not alone. Pretty much everyone who has children has gone through it as well. This is a time when the husband and wife will have some arguments, and both will have to make some real sacrifices. Just knowing this in advance is massively helpful. Know that you will have to take some time out for one another, to spend time together when you can get it. You need to have a date night once a week, every week. The same goes for when you have teenagers. The challenges are a little different, but just do not get blindsided by the fact that it is hard. There are some habits we can develop that can help us through these tough times.

One researcher found that a common characteristic of long, successful marriages was that the spouses said "I love you" to one another at least a couple of times a day. This seems like a small habit, but it yields enormous fruit. It seems love not spoken is not love at all. We all need to hear it as well as see it.

Another vital trait revealed by a wife who had been married a very long time was forgiveness. She thought a successful marriage was a marriage of two forgivers.[6] Forgiveness makes a lot of sense when you consider every marriage consists of a flawed person married to a flawed person in an imperfect world. Someone else said the ten rules of marriage are: communicate, communicate, communicate, communicate, admit the fault and say you're sorry, communicate, communicate, communicate, communicate, forgive. Often it takes a lot of communication to uncover the real problem so one spouse can lovingly confront and allow the other to take responsibility and forgive.

Forgiveness is one of those precepts that are easy to talk about and yet incredibly difficult to do. We all tend to keep a file cabinet full of all the offenses the other person has done. It is like this thing gets chained to our ankle, and we become comfortable with it, not realizing the weight is dragging us down. Another word for unforgiveness is bitterness. Medical researchers have found that unforgiveness/bitterness can even contribute to health problems. As some have said, it is like trying to get even with someone by drinking poison. We all need to ditch the file cabinet chained to our ankle and forgive people these petty offenses. Some things are more than petty and need exposure and confrontation, but we still need to release them. The old expression is true. When we all demand "an eye for an eye," it's not long before the whole world is blind.

I have already stated how important communication is, but I need to give some qualifiers here. Please understand some people are far better at communicating than others, and usually, the better ones are women. The younger a man is, the more he is wired for work or action. In fact, some say the male brain is not even fully developed until age 26. This must be true or how else would you get otherwise normal people to volunteer for combat (which is not all bad since we owe our freedom to this kind of bravery). Two days after my wife and I were married, we drove from Colorado to Phoenix to set up our first apartment together. I will never forget descending from the mountains about three hours out, deep in thought about something, and not needing to talk for about two hours. The silence seemed quite reasonable to me since we had just finished talking for what felt like forever leading up to that point. However, I am convinced my new wife was subconsciously testing me. She was wondering whether she had just married the Unabomber—because what kind of demented person would ever stay silent that long? Thankfully, the older I got, the more talkative I became. Concerning the differences between men and women, the French have a fabulous expression, "Vive la difference," meaning long live the difference. We do need to appreciate our differences, they are truly wonderful, and at the same time we need patience. Many women need a lot of patience concerning men's ability to communicate with them. But take heart, if I can learn, anyone can learn.

HANDLING CONFLICT

In describing his marriage, a favorite author of mine made a couple of statements that were particularly relevant to my situation. He said he was as ready for marriage as taking up the presidency—ditto.[7] The other quote was, "(marriage) is like taking Cinderella and Huck Finn and tossing them into a submarine, and closing the hatch. What did you think would happen?"[8] You will have conflict, and it only took me about 25 years to find out there are some good rules on how to fight. I will interject here that it would be extremely nice if wives would fight fair because their initial verbal advantage can leave men bewildered and speechless. But since fighting fair does not often happen in the heat of the moment, rules are fabulously helpful, if not essential.

Rule number one is to pick your battles wisely. Not every little thing is worth fighting over. Marriage involves a lot of give-and-take, a lot of compromises. It is beneficial not to personalize everything. Assume the other person has a good heart and merely has a different opinion you should respect. Usually, but not always, the person who has the strongest feelings about something is honored in the final decision. In my marriage, I figured out in a hurry that my wife, who was staying home with the kids, understood some family matters better than I did. However, there are times when things escalate, requiring the next rule.

Rule number two says that when it turns exceptionally heated, someone has to initiate the order of engagement. Take a deep breath and go sit down at the table. If one of the spouses is too angry to talk immediately, they may have to cool off somewhere until they are ready. When both parties are able to speak, the most offended spouse gets to speak first. The first person states the problem or the issues as they see them, and the other person listens. The listening person then has to repeat what the other person said until there is satisfaction that accurate communication has occurred. The second person then gets to speak and state their view of the problems and issues, and the other person has to repeat back what they said. Next, you both take a 5-to-10-minute break and sit down and repeat if necessary.[9] Couples can graduate into a shortened version once they realize good listening skills require them to repeat back what they think the other person is saying. The old expression goes, "sparks can burn the house down, or they can keep the hearth warm," and we would much prefer the latter.

Rule number three states that you do not let the sun go down on your anger. This might take some willpower, but you clearly must forgive and get over it by the end of the day. Things that stew for too long do not turn into anything pleasant. One habit I have developed over time is always hugging my wife the first time I see her at the beginning of the day. I make every effort to do this every day, whether there was a conflict or not. The funny thing is, there has not been as much conflict since I committed to doing this. We must always fight the temptation to think that the grass is greener somewhere else. The grass is greener where you water it.

WHAT ABOUT THE KIDS?

Since children, and how to raise them, are an obvious source of passionate discussion and sometimes conflict, I am going to mention a couple of essential bits of wisdom. I was driving the car one day and listening to the radio. A woman was discussing one of the most valuable pieces of knowledge she gained in her marriage. Someone revealed to her, or she discovered, that the children are not the center of the family. They are a welcome and incredibly loved addition to the family, but they are not the center of all attention and activity. Children, in fact, do not want the pressure of being the center of everything. Children should not have to handle that kind of pressure. They just want to be kids. Mom and dad's relationship is paramount because if mom and dad do not stay married, the children will end up far worse off. Just like men are wrong when they make their job an idol and more important than anything else, women are also wrong when elevating the children above everything else. We have already mentioned how absolutely important raising children is, but this will not turn out well if the marriage is not held in the highest esteem.

The next principle concerning children is necessary because it is so common sense and yet profound. The principle is this: do not let your kids do anything that makes you dislike them. The psychologist who advocates this says you first might want to check with your spouse to see if you are a fairly normal person.

If you are, and you do not like a particular behavior your child is exhibiting, nobody else will like it either. If you do not correct it, the world will; and the world is often ruthless. Believe it or not, young children can actually go out to a restaurant and act like human beings for 25 or 30 minutes when properly trained and guided by parents. There are many other things kids can do as well that are referred to as socialized behavior. Parents have a lot of tools at their disposal. For instance, knowing that 15 minutes in timeout for them feels more like 2 hours is the type of knowledge we can use to our advantage. When we put our minds to it, there are many ways to encourage children to act appropriately among other people. Children who do not learn to socialize well often have many problems throughout life. Parents are doing them a terrible disservice when they do not love them enough to guide and discipline them.[10]

Marriage and raising children are undoubtedly difficult, but is it worth it? All the data indicates the majority of married people are very happy and healthy. Author Tim Keller notes, "...by far the greatest percentage of divorces happen to those who marry before the age of 18, who have dropped out of high school, and who have had a baby together before marrying."[11] He goes on to say:

A 1992 study of retirement data shows that individuals who were continuously married had 75% more wealth at retirement than those who never married or who divorced and did not remarry...All surveys tell us that the number of married people who say they are "very happy" in their marriages is high–about 61-62%–and there has been little decrease in this figure during the last decade. Most striking of all, longitudinal studies demonstrate that two thirds of those unhappy marriages out there will become happy within five years if people stay married and do not get divorced. This led University of Chicago sociologist Linda J. Waite to say, "the benefits of divorce have been oversold."[12]

The last statistic is remarkable–two thirds of unhappy marriages become happy within five years if the couples stay together. Conversely, the divorce rates for second and third marriages are higher than for first marriages. The divorce rate is as high as 67% for second marriages and 73% for a third marriage.[13]

Life's difficult undertakings are often very worthwhile doing and sticking with it. The sticking with it part is much easier when you do life together with other couples and have friendships as well. I have met with a couple of other guys once a week for over 20 years, and they have been immensely instrumental in helping me through difficult times. We have to be intentional in our relationships. They are extremely important in every aspect of our life.

RELATIONSHIPS IN GENERAL

I have spent a lot of time in this chapter talking about marriage relationships but not much yet about singles. Marriage is not meant for everyone, and some of the people who have had the most significant impact on all of human history were not married. With that in mind, I will write a little about relationships in general.

As I said before, we all need friends, but some people have difficulty in establishing friendships. This may be due to disposition or upbringing, or any number of other things. Something not obvious, but very true nonetheless, concerning friendships is that the friendship itself has to be about something besides just the friendship. Otherwise, there is an intensity or neediness about it that it cannot withstand. This is why relationships often develop naturally among people who do common interests or activities together. Sometimes that occurs in the workplace, but other times friendships can develop from hobbies or volunteer activities that serve others. When we share experiences with other people, we tend to focus on others. It is sometimes easier to remember that to have a friend, you have to be a friend doing something fun or in common together.[14]

All of us have some issues, and some of those issues we bring from our growing up years because no one has had perfect parents. Parents are usually doing the best job they can, but you have to remember they also did not have perfect parents. One primary issue springs from growing up within a performance-based system. Because we are imperfect children, with tons to learn, we learn very quickly that if we do good things, life is good, and when we are bad, bad repercussions are on the way. Some of this is necessary, but it sets us up to feel like no one has ever loved us unconditionally. Conditional love does not feel like unconditional, real love. Even with good parents, it is difficult in life to feel real love, and so we try to get it any way we can to fill the void.[15] Some of the common ways we subconsciously try to get love include lying (these are usually little modifications of the truth so people will like us), attacking (anger is the most common because you can get what you want so quickly, but criticism and withdrawing approval also work), playing the victim (feigning injury to get sympathy, attention, or support), and clinging (excessive flattery, gratefulness or gift-giving).[16] There are many different manifestations of these four, but rather than get bogged down on every combination, here is the main subtle point. When you get what you think you want using these overt or subconscious methods, it never feels like love in the end because deep down you know it was purchased.[17] You end up feeling empty and unsatisfied and possibly not even knowing why. Then you find yourself doing some of the same things all over again in an endless cycle, pursuing what is missing in your life.

To break the cycle, consider the following two laws of relationships that are very helpful. The first law is the law of choice. This law is the most fundamental principle of all relationships; everyone has the right to choose what they say and do. A relationship is the natural result of people making independent choices. Relationships are like brushstrokes on canvas. They are all different and unique. And we can't make it a particular color by ourselves.[18] The second is the law of expectations. It says we never have the right to expect that another person will do anything for us. Expectations lead to disappointment, anger, and unhappiness in relationships. An exception to this is a spoken promise that all parties understand, in which case we can have some expectations.[19] I might add that these laws are stated with some caveats for spouses and children where there are limits on your choices because we do have expectations, such as fidelity. The laws still hold to a great extent because they are designed for people to feel safe. When children and even adult children are reluctant to have an open, honest conversation with a parent, there is a good chance they do not feel safe. Several of these relational attributes may lurk below the surface. This holds in all close relationships. People want to feel safe in their conversations with family and close friends.

Many of the principles or guidelines laid out in this chapter were learned the hard way by people who came before you. Some of you have already experienced some of the situations yourself. Others may question their validity, but at least we are starting the conversation. Much of this is about starting a conversation. Life is a gift and an adventure and should be lived accordingly without totally "contemplating our navels" over every relational interaction. Relationships, however, are so vital to our happiness that neither should we float along in life taking them for granted.

3

PERSONAL FINANCES

Finances Are Very Personal

YOU MAY HAVE NOTICED BY now that banks and merchants want you to have credit cards – and lots of them. They spend extraordinary amounts of money sending out flyers to your address and advertising on TV and other places trying to convince you to get their card. This should make you suspicious. Usually, when companies spend like that to advertise a financial product, it is because it is a whopping good deal for them; but for you, perhaps not so much. Unfortunately, we live in a world where you almost have to have a credit card, or you cannot rent a car and may have difficulty with other transactions as well. If nearly everyone has to have one, what can be so bad about them?

THE PROBLEM WITH CREDIT CARDS

The following statistic highlights the biggest single problem for younger consumers concerning credit cards. Consumers will spend up to 100% more using a credit card rather than cash or having the money come directly out of their bank account.[1] This means if you are in a store buying stuff with a credit card, you buy twice as much compared to if you paid with cash. Everyone wants to buy something shiny and new because they just know it will impress their friends, family, or people they do not even know (these people are not nearly as impressed as you might think) and in the process make themselves quite happy. This is what we call an emotional purchase. You want something, and you want it now, especially if that new thing will not affect your immediate ability to buy food or pay for rent and utilities. Studies show, however, that when you have to pay cash or have it come directly out of your account, you will spend far less. You spend far less because, in the back of your mind, you know there are some things you have to pay for soon. But if you can put it on the credit card, that is different. You can pay it off sometime in the distant future.

The problem is the future is never that distant when it comes to debt. In what seems like no time at all, there is a bill arriving in your mailbox. If you do not pay in full, you get to pay 17% interest on the remaining balance plus a late fee if you don't pay on time. This is depressing, of course. This is so depressing you may have to go out shopping, or at least out with friends. And so begins the cycle. The credit card company, the credit card network, and the payment processor are all happy, splitting up the 1.3%-3.4% processing fee on every purchase (as well as the credit card company raking it in with the 17% interest rate, late fees, and various other fees).[2] The merchant is happy because you spent far more in their store or on their website than you would have otherwise. On the other hand, you can eventually find yourself in some very substantial high-interest debt and more depressed than you ever thought possible. This all of a sudden has become very personal.

Emotional, immediate purchases rob you of the ability to make wise decisions with your money. When people are forced to delay a purchase, they will walk out of the store, or leave the shopping website, and eventually, start thinking about whether they really want or need the desired item. If a person does decide they want the product, then they can start saving for it. While saving, they start realizing just how many hours they have to work to buy what they so desperately want. They might also do a little more research on the best product to buy. In the middle of all this, the transmission may go out in their car. You can definitely see why merchants want you to buy now.

Credit cards also steal a certain amount of long-term joy. There is something about working and saving up for some desired item and looking forward to its purchase. This is because we are becoming goal-focused when we do so. Setting goals and achieving them gives us a great deal of long-term satisfaction.

The reason I can speak somewhat knowledgeably about credit cards is because I've been there and done that. Many of us have picked up these lessons the hard way, and we want to spare you some of the pain. When you learn too many things the hard way, life can get hard and stay hard. When I was younger and did not have much money in the bank, I finally learned that grabbing a credit card out of the wallet is like holding onto a piece of bloody, raw meat while paddleboarding in a tank full of sharks—because you are.

HOW TO SAY NO

The temptation to get into debt is fed significantly by our consumer culture. A huge component of that culture is a massive amount of advertising enticing us to buy products by appealing to our vanity or emotions. Extensive advertising is apparently very effective. An awareness of advertising techniques helps combat the message always to consume (a state-of-the-art DVR to filter out commercials is a godsend).

We might need something else as well. There was a very famous experiment conducted by a Stanford researcher starting in the 1960s called the marshmallow experiment. Children between the ages of four and five were told they could have a marshmallow and eat it immediately, or they could wait a little while (up to 20 minutes) and get two marshmallows or other preferred treats.[3] Many of the kids agonized over the decision. Some ate it immediately, and others waited in order to get an additional marshmallow. The researchers then tracked the children over 40 years. They found that the ones who delayed had far more positive life outcomes like higher SAT scores, lower substance abuse, and better social skills. More recent experiments show that the results may have been magnified by not taking into account the parents' socio-economic background, the parents' educational level, or the reliability of their environment. However, the overall results are hard to dispute.[4]

Delayed gratification allows people to study for a test instead of hitting the bars, eating healthy food later rather than junk food now, or putting off a purchase to have money in the bank account so as not to build debt. The simple discipline of delayed gratification is something all parents should try to instill in their children. There are even methods available online for boosting delayed gratification disciplines in adults if they were not taught them as children. The ability to postpone a purchase will help us avoid buying a bunch of plastic crap that ends up in landfills (or the Pacific trash vortex). Future generations may someday call the time we live in now the age of landfill consumerism. I'm just saying maybe we should think about our purchases, cut our personal debt, and spare the landfill.

We might also want to reflect on what actually makes us happy. We build mental pictures in our mind projecting some seemingly cheerful scene in the future with us in the center of it doing something fun. We daydream about some activity or circumstance "out there" as being far better than our circumstances in the here and now. There is nothing wrong with dreaming as long as we keep some perspective. In the following two scenarios, who is ultimately happier? The first one consists of a regular guy up north fishing and camping with two close friends sitting in an inexpensive tent streaming football as they banter and joke as only good friends can. The other scene is some dude bombing to Bimini in a boat he can ill afford with so-called friends aboard he will never see again if things ever start going bad. I will put my money on the regular guy with a good friend or two.

Sometimes we should perhaps refocus and be thankful for what we have. I'm not saying that we never buy a nice boat or car or whatever else. We should just remember material stuff won't ultimately make us happy and, therefore, never worth the headaches of debt. Save your money and pay cash for whatever has wheels or floats on water or any other substantially depreciating item. You will be glad you did.

LESS RUINOUS TYPES OF DEBT

Now that I have your attention concerning debt, you may wonder if all indebtedness is ruinous. The best rule concerning debt is to have the least amount necessary. There are times when it is difficult to avoid having some debt, such as when paying for education, buying a house, or starting a business.

Education is generally considered a wise investment. Not all of us come from households where we could count on help once we graduated from high school and wanted to pursue college. Some ways to minimize education debt include scouring the landscape for scholarships and looking into military educational opportunities. Once you have exhausted these sources, you can look into the possibility of living at home while attending a local junior college or doing online courses for the first two years and then transferring to the school of your choice for the last two years. There is also nothing wrong with working while you are attending college. Some employers look very favorably upon job candidates who have the discipline and drive to work their way through college. Even after doing all these things, you may still need to get some loans. Again, the goal is to get the best degree in the field you want to study with the least expense—the more marketable the degree, the more debt you can probably afford to take. The situation to avoid at all costs is the $200,000 degree in art history (or equivalent) that qualifies you after graduation to work as a server in the local boutique coffee shop. We should all remember that some things are fantastic as hobbies, but they will not pay the bills or your college debt.

Hopefully, when you get out on your own, your debt will not preclude you from buying a house if you so desire. There are many variables in determining how large a mortgage a person can afford, and there is not enough space to cover them all. When you shop for a loan, any loan officer can look at your income, assets, and debt level to quickly determine the maximum mortgage appropriate for your circumstances. There is always the temptation to go right to the max because we all know the house is an asset, right? Some of Robert Kiyosaki's best advice in his book *Rich Dad Poor Dad* is directed primarily at home buyers when he says an asset is something that you own where if you lose your job it makes you money. A house definitely does not meet these criteria because you still have to pay on the PITI (principal, interest, taxes, and insurance) when you lose your job. Even if you own the home outright, you will still pay taxes, property insurance, upkeep, lawn maintenance, and utilities. Assets are better looked at as things such as rental properties that have a positive cash flow, stocks and bonds, and latchkey businesses that do not require your every waking moment to run them. If we were to lose our jobs, those things would actually generate income.[5]

We all need to live somewhere, and so we may want to buy a house someday. Just do not overdo it and become house poor, thinking you have this wonderful asset. Many successful people choose to live in modest residences until they own enough real assets to afford a nicer residence. I realize there are many factors in buying a house, such as the local school system's quality, safety, and commute distance. The main point to remember is to keep your mortgage manageable because your house is not a piggy bank.

Starting a business is another life event you may find requires more cash than you have on hand. Starting your own business is definitely a worthwhile endeavor since enduring businesses serve the needs of other people. A business can also provide you with an income. The keyword here is "enduring." Twenty percent of businesses fail the first year, and up to 50% fail after 5 years. Entrepreneurs are generally not discouraged by these statistics because we all learn a tremendous amount in our failures, perhaps more than our successes.

Nonetheless, we obviously want to multiply our chances for success, and with new businesses, this means having enough cash on hand. Starting a first-time business may be the only situation where I would recommend a person consider getting a loan (even if it is a small one) in order to bring a local business bank alongside as your advisor. The first question they will ask is, "Where is your business plan?" This question could broadside people who did not major in business in college or do not have business experience. These days, though, you can do some research online and figure out how to put together a business plan. A good local banker can give you tremendous insight into your plan's strength, local market conditions, finances, contacts, and on and on. I have no involvement in the banking industry. Still, I have certainly had experience watching people try to start businesses with no help from others who could have given fantastic advice. Again, as with the two previous situations, the wise move is to not get in over your head in debt.

Unfortunately, many people attempt to start their own business by begging money from relatives. In a way, asking help from family members looks like a reasonable request since we rely on the family in times of need, but in this situation, beware. If your extended family provides too much help, then one is less likely to solicit help from local banks who will demand a business plan and, at the same time, offer a lot of good advice. Also, if you default to the bank, you sour the relationship with the bank. But when you fail to pay your family back, you spoil the relationship with the family. Some families refuse to finance other family members primarily for this reason. Partnerships are another area that can damage relationships. Business arrangements with non-family members are tricky enough since someone usually needs to own 51% to make final decisions legally, and no one may have spelled this out. But with family member partnerships, you enter a whole new realm of difficulty. Your spoken or unspoken expectations based on relational familiarity can cause trouble down the road. The only way you should ever enter a partnership, and especially family partnerships, is to have everything in writing upfront. In this case, "spoken" is not good enough. Violating this principle has destroyed numerous relationships.

I am not trying to write a finance book or a business manual. I am trying to highlight some financial considerations people can bear in mind to avoid an enormous amount of misery. Millennials and Xers, especially need to gain financial wisdom quickly since some of them find themselves sandwiched between the great recession and COVID 19. As mentioned in the previous chapter, financial problems are one of the primary stressors in marriage and thus necessitate discussion alongside any discussion on relationships. In our consumer culture, debt is the primary financial hazard lurking to entrap us. Perhaps I should say imprison us. If having money gives us a certain amount of freedom, then having a lot of debt is the opposite. In little time, substantial debt makes you feel like someone put you on a giant hamster wheel in a cage. You run faster and faster with little hope of ever going anywhere or getting out as the light at the end of the tunnel darkens. You would love to go somewhere and do something fun, but the bills just keep coming. Arguments ensue, and unfortunately, relationships get strained.

If you are already in this kind of situation, there is hope. Author and radio host Dave Ramsey started advising people with debt problems in 1992 and has a system that has stood the test of time. He has helped millions of people get out of serious debt. I encourage you to go to his website and to read his book.

You will discover the exact debt you should pay off first and in what order.[6] His system also teaches you how to make a budget, establish an emergency fund, and successive steps to achieve financial independence. As with anything worthwhile, initially, there are some sacrifices, but the outcome is worth it ten times over. I have no affiliation with Dave Ramsey in any way. I just recognize that he has probably helped more marriages than anyone in our country by educating so many people about getting out of debt and handling finances responsibly.

INVESTING IN THE HUMBLE CASINO

The last thing I will bring up in the realm of finance is investing. Most people have the option to invest in some form of IRA or 401(k). Since these investments are allowed to grow tax-free, they are a fantastic opportunity for everyone. However, for many people, these financial instruments appear a little confusing, or they don't have the self-confidence to determine where the investments should go. The investment landscape even looks somewhat risky, and there is a fear that the experts will beat you at this game. The whole thing might also remind you of playing Vegas. There are some similarities to Las Vegas, but there does not have to be. An illustration may help you see what is going on.

Suppose you had $6,000 to spend, and you decide to fly to Las Vegas and play the casinos. You catch a van from the airport into town. As you drive on major highways and cross numerous busy intersections, you notice the town has grown considerably. The city is now like a mini Los Angeles, with bigger and better casinos everywhere. You mention to the driver, "Wow, I can't believe they can build all this if the people are winning." The driver solemnly answers, "I assure you the people are not winning in the long run. The house always wins in the long term and gets its cut. Federal, state, and local governments always get their cut. But there are not that many dollars that leave Las Vegas compared to how many come in." For some reason, you start wondering if this is a great idea. You decide to investigate whether there is a different kind of casino available. One that is not decorated and furnished extravagantly with everyone's lost money.

You walk around for a long time and finally see a modest little green building called the Humble Casino. Intrigued, you go inside and find a person at the counter and ask them why their casino is so different looking. "Well," she says, "we are a little strange. You see, if you put your money down on our preferred game, you bet on how the top 500 companies in the United States perform. We traditionally pay you 9.6% annually if you leave the money alone and don't play any other games, constantly withdrawing to play the other bets. If you keep coming back and add to it, all the other money also accumulates at that same percentage rate and tends to snowball into large amounts year after year, called compounding. And we only charge you $.20 per thousand dollars. If you put your full $6,000 in our casino, we would only charge you $1.20, about half the cost of a regular coffee across the street. However, we are humble and don't like to encourage get-rich-quick schemes. If you come in all the time and bet your money on individual companies, we will add lots of fees. We assure you that you will not time your buying and selling decisions very well. You will make a lot less than 9.6% annually. In fact, if you constantly buy and sell, placing bets on individual companies, we will begin to resemble all the other casinos down the street, and you will more than likely lose a lot of earning potential."

After thinking about this a couple of seconds, you decide to put your $6,000 down on the Humble Casino's preferred game. Next year, you decide to put another $6,000 down, and the year after. In fact, every year you decide this is the game you like to play because, at the 10-year point, they tell you your balance is $117,821. They even tell you that if you go online, you can find an investment calculator that will tell you at 20 years you should have around $397,480; at 30 years, about $1,096,894; and at 40 years about $2,846,096.[7] If you factor in inflation, historically around 3%, you will have less than these numbers in real buying power. At 30 years, inflation-adjusted, you would have $603,206, and at 40 years, you would have $1,230,000 in today's buying power. That is still impressive considering it is only $250 a pay period (if paid twice a month). If you could ever afford $1,000 a month you would have after 30 years about $2,190,000 ($1,206,000 inflation-adjusted) and at 40 years you would have $5,690,000 ($2,450,000 inflation-adjusted). You decide you really like the Humble Casino. Now you know why they painted it green—it pays like a cash register.

The Humble Casino is actually a stock brokerage firm (like E*TRADE, Fidelity, Charles Schwab, or your company-sponsored plan). The preferred game is buying Fortune 500 mutual funds like Schwab's S&P 500 index (SWPPX) or Fidelity's 500 index (FXAIX). The *index* in this case is an average value of the Fortune 500 companies and investing in them, or a group of stocks, is often called *indexing*. These funds allow you to buy into the top 500 companies in the United States and charge only .02%. Several other companies, such as Vanguard, offer similar products, and their expense ratios are comparable. I have no affiliation with any of these companies. Another terrific attribute of these index funds is how easily a person diversifies. You do not have all your eggs in one basket. You immediately spread your investment over 500 companies.

Why did I choose a 9.6% growth annually in my example? Doesn't the stock market fluctuate all over the place? The best way to look at the market performance is to consider the stock market index as two different lines. The one-line swings up and down over time wildly and looks like an erratic EKG. This line is the short term view of the market based on fear and greed. The market continues to head down, so the crowd gets scared and finally sells; or the stock market goes up over a long period, so the crowd feels like they are missing out and eventually buys. Herd instinct can drive the market wildly up and down. Unfortunately, the crowd usually shows up late and gets slaughtered.

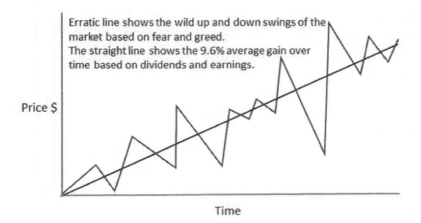

The other stock market line (the same line averaged over many years) is the long term index that shows a continuous increase of 9.6% per year from 1900 to 2006.[8] Some sources like to quote a total market gain between 10 and 11% per year from 1926 to 2018.[9] I like the more conservative number of 9.6%.

The 9.6% average gain per year held through two world wars, a great depression, an Arab oil embargo, and numerous other events. This nice long increasing line is the stock market index based on earnings and dividends. This is the reason why the preferred game involves putting the money in and never touching it. If you are continually buying and selling and moving your money around, you eventually get hammered by mistiming market volatility. Just like the casinos where the house gets to keep a certain percentage, brokerages also charge fees and make more money on constant buying and selling.

In the above example, the reason I chose $6,000 invested annually is that $500 a month yields $6,000 for the year. There are many people who, if they eliminated their short-term debt and debt on depreciating assets, could easily afford a $500 a month investment. The best way to invest is to have the money come directly from your paycheck every payday and go straight into your chosen investment. This is also called dollar-cost averaging and ensures that you will buy during market lows and highs so that over time you match the overall market performance. You do not worry about a substantial market downturn. In fact, the younger you are, the less you are bothered by a market plunge because effectively you end up buying stocks at a discount when the market is down. Even when you buy when stocks are high, you know prices eventually come down to average everything out.

So, what about the experts who know how to time the market? No one knows how to time the market. You should repeat the phrase to yourself many times until it finally sinks in. There is no expert, and there is no computer program that knows what is going to happen tomorrow. That is why no one can time the market. Sometimes the experts get lucky over a run of 5 to 10 years, but the data proves few people beat the stock market average over long periods. By indexing, you will beat 85% of all the experts over 20 years.[10] You will beat an even higher percentage of experts over 30 years or more. The fees and ill-timed market dips always catch up with them. Do not be tempted to invest in funds with high expense ratios or with experts that charge hefty fees. They will more than likely do worse than the average market performance over time. If they charged just 1%, it would cost you $200,989 over 30 years. No, you did not misread this. 1% in fees will cost you a little over $200,000 at the end of 30 years when investing $6,000 a year. Because of the powerful force of compounding, 8.6% only produces $895,805 versus 9.6% yielding $1,096,894. Fees add up fast.

I am not suggesting that you should not have a financial advisor. A good financial advisor can help you establish your financial goals, keep you on track and disciplined, and help with tax laws and insurance decisions. I am suggesting, though, that your advisor should charge a straightforward fee and not a percentage of your investment. They also should not get a kickback from the investments they advise people to buy. Advisors can also give you great advice on allocation based on your age. When you are young, you can risk having a lot of your portfolio in S&P 500 index stock funds; but as you get older, you need to have a certain amount in something like an intermediate bond fund that is less risky. Some people may also want to have a small percentage in an international index fund, emerging-market fund, or a REIT (Real Estate Investment Trust) fund to diversify further. You can also educate yourself by buying an easy to read investment book like John Bogle's *The Little Book of Common Sense Investing*. This book is so simple, yet profound, I recommend everyone read it.

One of the most fantastic aspects of this type of investing is the amount of passivity. Your money automatically comes out of your paycheck and into your IRA or 401(k) allocated to an index fund with the lowest expense ratio possible. You do nothing else. Soon you are free to reflect upon how wonderful it is not to owe on credit cards and other things you do not need. You finally have time, money, and energy to go out and do some fun things with family and friends. You notice how you and your spouse have far fewer arguments than ever before. Work even seems to have more meaning and purpose since most of your paycheck does not go to digging yourself out of a hole. You have this intense desire to tell those you care about how not to ruin their personal life with financial debt.

4

POLITICS

Can We Be Civil?

I WAS HAVING DINNER RECENTLY with several coworkers in Johannesburg, South Africa. For some reason, quite a few of the restaurants in downtown Johannesburg give a couple of free bottles of wine with dinner. The only thing I can think of is that perhaps there is tremendous competitive pressure due to the abundance of good restaurants in the area. After we had all started dinner and had a glass of wine, the discussion drifted into politics. Soon, the guy on my right was yelling, perhaps screaming is a better word, at the guy on my left. I finally had to raise my voice to get everyone's attention (we were all pretty much equal coworkers) and asked them to tone it down some. I interjected that tolerance requires disagreement, or there is nothing to tolerate. It is OK for us to disagree with one another in a polite and reasonable manner, and each person is free to form their own opinion within the forum of private and public debate. They all stopped talking for a moment, looked around at one another, and then continued to have a very normal and polite conversation the rest of the evening, even though they talked politics.

People are surprised when you remind them that tolerance requires disagreement, or there is nothing to tolerate because within the last few decades, some people have confused tolerance to mean you have to agree with them. Within the context of a conversation, tolerance is the quality of allowing others to say what they like even if you do not agree or approve of what they are saying.[1] If you shout someone down and do not allow them to speak because you disagree with what they are saying, you are actually intolerant. I am not sure where the confusion originated, but this whole scenario definitely reveals how important a word's meaning is. I have found this singular technique of explaining tolerance has made it possible to have reasonable conversations on numerous occasions involving people from both sides of the political spectrum. There is only one main exception.

THE BIGOTRY OF NOT ALLOWING DISAGREEMENT

When told tolerance requires disagreement, or there is nothing to tolerate, there are a few people who answer with something like, "Well, I am not going to tolerate your bigotry, you hater!" When this happens, you need to pause, collect yourself, and calmly state, "Sig Heil, das ist die Fuhrer," because you have just encountered the ultimate, purest form of bigotry and the domain of dictators everywhere. We simply call this the bigotry of non-disagreement. You are absolutely not allowed to disagree with them about their pet cause or belief. They feel those who disagree with them must be silenced immediately by yelling, interrupting, and name-calling. All bigotry holds the rights of others they do not like in contempt.[2] They are attempting to annihilate your freedom of speech, and they will try to remove as many of your other rights as possible.

I don't know why so many people back down when they en-counter the bigotry of non-disagreement. I assume most people are just surprised and taken aback. Many people associate the definition of bigotry with racial and religious prejudice. Bigotry also means prejudice towards those who disagree with you. One of the most pronounced forms of prejudice is the act of silencing someone. When you think about it, these people are exercising the ultimate form of bigotry as they call you a bigot for merely offering up a different opinion. Lenin, Stalin, and Mao would all stand in hearty approval of such in-your-face hypocrisy. You should always call it out for what it is. If they do not acknowl-edge the truth, you will have to announce to others present what has just happened and why further discussion is impossible. A person cannot have a normal conversation with a tyrant.

The tyranny of forced agreement is the hallmark of dicta-tors, and the consequent next step is compelled speech. After they silence you, then they try to tell you what you must say. There is a vast difference between what you cannot say and what you must say. We actually do have some laws that restrict free-dom of speech. A person is not allowed to libel, slander, falsely advertise, or falsely yell fire in a crowded theater. However, compelled speech dictates what a person must say. Thankfully, the protection against compelled speech was upheld (except for very narrowly defined circumstances) by the US Supreme Court in West Virginia State Board Of Education vs. Barnette (1943). We should not take for granted the rights guaranteed by the Constitution and Bill of Rights and safeguard them at every opportunity.

Many people today seem to have a pet cause or belief, and these beliefs can vary profusely. Who knows, before long some-one's pet belief may include everyone having the right to marry

multiple wives or multiple husbands. We should be able to po-
litely disagree with them in public or private conversation and
give our opinion on the damaging social consequences of such
practices without being attacked or called a hater. We are not
judging them; we are judging their ideas. Remember, we do not
tolerate harmful actions, but we do tolerate different opinions in
our conversations. Typically, if we keep in mind some ground
rules, we can have a good and fruitful debate concerning a multitude of topics. The best ideas can have an opportunity to carry
the day.

NEVER UNDERESTIMATE THE POWER OF INCENTIVE

In our political discussions, we help ourselves when we acknowledge that both sides usually want to help others who are in
need. We differ in our assessment as to what methods best help
people. The old fishing example illustrates the difference; one
side believes you should give a person a fish, and then when they
are able, teach them how to fish. The other side also believes in
giving someone a fish when in need, teaching them how to fish,
and giving them the incentive to fish. The motivation part of this
is crucial concerning human behavior.

A favorite joke told by the citizens of the former Soviet
Union helps us see how incentive impacts us. Ivan gets up one
day and decides he would like to sign up for a car. He walks
down to the Bureau and enters the front door. He strolls over to
a desk where a bureaucrat is seated and states, "I want to sign
up for a car." The bureaucrat answers firmly, "Put your name
on the list; it will be a 10-year wait." Ivan thinks for a moment
and asks, "Will that be morning or afternoon?" The bureaucrat

exclaims, "Who cares, it's 10 years from now!" Ivan responds, "Well, the plumber is coming that morning."[3]

And that sums it up pretty succinctly. When people get paid the same whether they work or not, there is little motivation to build cars or fix plumbing. When they stood in long lines to buy sausage, the former Soviet citizens also used to say that the workers pretend to work and the government pretends to pay them. People tend to work when there is motivation to do so. We can look at history and our own experiences to see that this is true.

Socialism was first tried in our country when the pilgrims arrived. *Bradford's History of the Plymouth Settlement* details how the original governing contract stipulated that the settlers would all go out and work the community land together and then reap the benefits together. Their initial harvest was poor, so they tried to figure out how to make it better:

So they began to consider how to raise more corn, and obtain a better crop than they had done, so that they might not continue to endure the misery of want. At length after much debate, the governor, with the advice of the chief among them, allowed each man to plant corn for his own household, and to trust to themselves for that; in all other things to go on in the general way as before. So every family was assigned a parcel of land, according to the proportion of their number with that in view, – for present purposes only and making no division for inheritance, – all boys and children being included under some family. This was very successful. It made all hands very industrious, so that much more corn was planted than otherwise would have been by any means the governor

or any other could devise, and saved him a great deal
of trouble, and gave far better satisfaction. The women
now went willingly into the field, and took their little
ones with them to plant corn, while before they would al-
lege weakness and inability; and to have compelled them
would have been thought great tyranny and oppression.[4]

He writes further that the single men were also more motivated
since before they thought all their efforts were going towards
feeding other men's families without them receiving any benefit
in return. Incentive was restored.

Few people in our country are aware Communist China has a
similar incident in their history. I was in Shanghai recently, a few
months before the coronavirus, when an article in one of the local
newspapers caught my eye. When Mao came to power in China
in 1949, he abolished private property and made farmers live on
communal land (like what the Mayflower compact tried to do only
on a massive scale). By 1978 many of the farmers were starving
to death. In one village, they decided to buck the system and let
everyone secretly work their own designated land. I was intrigued
by this and did a little further research when I got back home. I
found this article in the *Wall Street Journal* chronicling the event:

Forty years ago this spring, corn farmers in Xiaogang
village, in the central province of Anhui (where Pearl
Buck set "The Good Earth"), reported a grain yield of 66
metric tons. This single harvest equaled the village's total output between 1955 and 1970—but for once the figure was not exaggerated. In fact, villagers underreported
their actual yield by a third, fearing officials would not
believe their record haul.

What caused this massive spike in production? A new fertilizer or hybrid seed? Better equipment? A catchy, rhymed propaganda slogan? No; Xiaogang's farmers were starving. After taking power in 1949, China's Communist Party had effectively abolished private land ownership, grouping farms into "people's communes" subservient to the state. By 1978 villages were crippled by quotas that seized most of what they grew for redistribution.

Only that season, there was no food. Xiaogang's farmers dug up roots, boiled poplar leaves with salt, and ground roasted tree bark into flour. Families left their thatched-roof homes and took to the road to beg.

On the night of Nov. 24, 1978, a farmer named Yan Hongchang summoned the heads of the village's desperate families to a clandestine meeting. On paper torn from a child's school workbook, the farmers wrote a 79-word pledge to divide the commune's land into family plots, submit the required quota of corn to the state, and keep the rest for themselves.

In 1624 Pilgrims in the American colonies attempted a similar reform: after two years of food shortages at Plymouth, the settlement abandoned communal farming for family plots. People worked harder than before, with women and children joining men in the field. The colony never starved again.

But American Pilgrims did not fear charges of sedition. "In the case of failure," the Xiaogang farmers' pledge concluded, "we are prepared for death or prison, and other commune members vow to raise our children until they are 18 years old." Then they signed their names.

By springtime the commune's chief said the group had "dug up the cornerstone of socialism," and threatened severe punishment. But a cadre above him eyed the record harvest—and a 20-fold increase in annual family income. The official told Mr. Yan he would protect Xiaogang and the rebellious farmers, so long as their experiment didn't spread.

But villagers gossip. Farmers talk about their fields. The grass-roots experiment did spread. In Beijing, three years after Mao Zedong's death, Deng Xiaoping urged the Chinese to ignore political dogma and instead "seek truth from facts." Now came news that dissenting farmers were actually growing food.

This year marks the 40th anniversary of Deng's decision to scrap collective farming. In its place came one of the country's most popular reforms, the Household Contract Responsibility System, or *chengbao,* which allows families to farm their own allocation of land and sell most of the harvest at unregulated prices.

In today's revisionist China, Xiaogang village is a "red tourism" attraction, albeit the only one whose "patriotic education base" (museum) celebrates local defiance of government policy. Its exhibition hall displays a copy of the farmers' pledge—the original was lost years ago—and floor-to-ceiling photographs of its signatories. The men are lauded as heroes, and Xiaogang celebrated with a slogan: "The origin of our nation's economic rise!"[5]

That single year's harvest in 1978 exceeded all the corn production from 1955 through 1970! All because the farmers planted and harvested on their own plots. Incentive makes a huge difference.

Many students today say they like socialism, but I do not think this is necessarily true because they mostly all respond to the following scenario the same way. Suppose that you are taking a class and working exceptionally hard and have a solid A. Trevor is taking the same class and having the time of his life, never studying, and currently has an F. The professor wants to make your A a C to bring Trevor's F up to a C and yet still keep the mean average of the class the same. Are you OK with this arrangement? Almost everyone I present this scenario to unanimously answers "no" because it is not fair. They instinctively know that this arrangement is bad for them, bad for Trevor, and bad for us.

Society suffers when people are rewarded for lazy or immature behavior. The immature or lazy person suffers when they do not learn to better themselves through hard work and discipline. The person who has the A lowered to a C suffers because they are not rewarded for their hard work. They also know that without that reward, they would not have the motivation to work as hard in the future and thus would be cheating themselves of the opportunity to gain more knowledge and improve themselves. Incentive is crucial.

Someone might complain that my previous examples resemble communism more than socialism. As of this writing, a leading candidate for one of the party's presidential nominations states on his website that he plans on passing free housing for all, Medicare for all, free college for all, mostly nationalizing the energy sector, and massively expanding Social Security, among other things.[6] He calls himself a democratic socialist. Yet, I do not see how this differs much from communism except that he has not outright banned private ownership (yet). However, the amount of government takeover he advocates is still quite stunning.

The amount of taxation required for such programs is also stunning. In the previous chapter, concerning debt, I stated that not having any discretionary income is like slavery because you have very little freedom. People who have lived under socialist regimes will tell you massive taxation has the same effect. When you work hard and yet do not have money left to travel, go to sporting events, restaurants, or make decisions for your family's benefit, then someone has taken your freedom.[7]

When you point some of these things out to a democratic socialist, they will tell you that it will not be that bad because they are trying to emulate the Scandinavian countries. The Scandinavian countries are free enterprise systems and, in many ways, have fewer restrictions on businesses than we have. Most of Europe has had free healthcare for quite some time as well. That is perhaps easily accomplished when someone else (the United States) has paid for much of their national defense umbrella over the last 70 years.

When you are in your 20s or 30s, it is quite popular to believe that extensively taxing the rich is a great idea. What I am about to say is extremely important. That so-called "rich person" you want to enormously tax is you in 20 or 30 years from now if you work hard and lead a responsible life. No one seems to tell you this simple little fact, but it is true. There just are not enough of the super-rich to provide the trillions in tax revenue they need, so they always have to go after those who have more modest assets. If you work diligently and take care of your family and try to do the right thing, you will more than likely have some assets and the ability to enjoy some part of your retirement in a few decades. Unless, of course, they punish you for working hard and leading a responsible life.

People who work diligently and lead responsible lives are predominantly the ones who give you excellent medical care and cure diseases, build roads and other infrastructure, build or repair your car or home, work at businesses that serve your needs, grow food and get it to your local supermarket, and on and on. When you punish the people who bring you these things, prepare to become Venezuela.

VENEZUELA AND ARGENTINA

Venezuela was the wealthiest country in South America from 1958 through the 1980s. This was largely due to its tremendous oil reserves. But something started to happen in the latter part of the 1980s and culminated with where they are today; that something is socialism. There was an increasing government take-over of industry, and of course, it peaked with Hugo Chavez and his successor, Nicholas Maduro. Bret Stephens of the *New York Times* summarizes Venezuela's situation:

> Government overspending created catastrophic deficits when oil prices plummeted. Worker co-ops wound up in the hands of incompetent and corrupt political cronies. The government responded to its budgetary problems by print-ing money, leading to inflation. Inflation led to price con-trols, leading to shortages. Shortages led to protests, leading to repression and the destruction of democracy. Thence to widespread starvation, critical medical shortages, an explo-sion in crime, and a refugee crisis to rival Syria's.

All of this used to be obvious enough, but in the age of Alexandria Ocasio-Cortez, it has to be explained all over again. Why does socialism never work? Because, as Margaret Thatcher explained, "eventually you run out of other people's money."[8]

And you always run out of other people's money. That money you run out of—it came from people working hard because they had incentive. When you punish hard-working people via government takeover of large parts of the economy and massive taxation, those hard-working people soon stop performing. One tragic result of all this was the average citizen of Venezuela losing 24 pounds of weight in 2017 (the last year accurate data was available).[9] You can rest assured that Chavez and Maduro never lost any weight as they accumulated billions in personal wealth. Socialism always kills creativity and entrepreneurial skills, takes money from the hard-working, and enriches government bureaucrats. The joke on the street in Venezuela was that socialism loves poor people so much it multiplies them.

Argentina is another fine example of socialistic policies ruining a nation in our hemisphere. Few people realize that Argentina was one of the top 10 wealthiest countries in the world at the end of the 19th century due to productive farmland, abundant mineral resources, and a great climate. In 1913 it had a per capita income higher than France and twice that of Italy. Both conservative and liberal politicians have made a mess of things since then, but the overall trend has always been towards more governmental control of the economy. From 2007 to 2015, there was more government expansion. The value of the Argentinian peso fell from one dollar in 2001 to eight cents in 2015 as government expenditures exceeded 40% of GDP. Today, the peso is worth less than two cents.[10]

If the incentive destroying attributes of socialism are so obvious, why does it remain popular among a portion of the population? One reason is that crafty politicians have figured out that socialistic promises appeal to unsuspecting people and, therefore, are an avenue for gaining power. There is a subtle and deceptive strategy that goes along with this. The first component of the plan is to demonstrate a violation of some arbitrary standard of fairness. I say arbitrary because standards of fairness vary significantly among people. There is no such thing as perfectly fair in real life. Let's say they determine that it is not fair that everyone does not have free food, free medical care, and free housing. The next step is to dream up some utopian system that will give everyone all these things. All you have to do is trust them and their brilliance and compassion, and all these things will be theirs. The problem is always the same, though. Utopian systems never exist in the real world. That is why they are called utopias.

In the real world, as we have seen, you get something like the cartoon in the Wizard of Id. A presidential candidate stands on the king's balcony addressing the subjects (voters) and says, "Elect me, and I promise you free healthcare!" and everyone cheers. Next he says, "Free housing! Free clothing!" and everyone cheers. Next he says, "Food stamps!" and everyone cheers again. Lastly he says, "And jobs for everybody! Any questions?" There is silence. Finally, one of the subjects asks, "Who needs jobs?"[11] As we have seen, this begins the downward slide.

FREEDOM IS GOOD

Utopian ideals like socialism never work in the real world because they do not account for how people truly act and live their lives. In a world that consists of imperfect people, we need a system that maximizes freedom and yet motivates people to serve one another through their work. For the most part, we have that system in the United States and have had it for the last several hundred years. It is called the free enterprise system combined with our constitutional form of government.

Freedom is a good thing. We know this is true because no one ever said give me slavery or give me death. Patrick Henry's famous quote did state, however, "...give me liberty, or give me death!" Unfortunately, we take freedom for granted, and I think we take the free enterprise system for granted as well. The "free" in free enterprise refers to consumers' freedom to buy what they would like and the freedom of people to own and start businesses they would like without much government interference. This results in businesses of various sizes, competing with one another to sell a product or service that consumers want to buy. Competition is good because it sparks creativity, which in turn leads to new and fabulous products. Competition leading to creativity is why you can choose different varieties of cell phones, cars, clothes, computers, furniture, appliances, houses, and hundreds of other products. You also can choose from an array of musicians, artists, doctors, restaurants, workout facilities, dry cleaners, and hair salons. If anyone charges too much or has an inferior product, fewer people buy what they have to offer. If there is a lot of demand for a product or service, then more people enter that business and produce that product, which eventually brings the price down. The price is set where the supply and demand curves intersect. There are literally millions of decisions made by free people every day that automatically determine the production of future goods, services, and prices. No central government could ever do this. When you have a government entity dictating goods and services, you may end up with one model of car. If history repeats itself, everyone may also have to like the same color.

Centralized economies have little idea of the number of products or services to produce. You get the amount of electrical power they decide you should have, and you get the quantity and quality of doctors they decide you should have. Oh, and I almost forgot, you get to have the surgery when they decide you should get it. At least everyone gets the same lousy power grid and the same horrible medical care. Except for government officials, theirs is substantially better. If you like the idea of fairness meaning everyone gets the same inferior goods and services, then socialism may be for you.

The unmotivated and uncreative tide lowers everyone down to the same low standard. The free enterprise system believes the tide rises and brings everyone up to a higher standard of living. This is exactly what we have seen in our own country over the last several hundred years. The United States is the most charitable country in the world. Our economic system produces abundance which allows us to give to people in need throughout the world. We have the ability and freedom to support the arts as well.

Some people are unaware that the quality and amount of goods and services produced are not a fixed entity. Productive and competitive free enterprise systems provide more goods and services, and this makes everyone better off. Yes, we do have the Pareto principle problem, which points to certain people excelling in their field and thus gaining a greater share of wealth. However, many of those people also employ hundreds or thousands and have to meet payroll. They also are rewarded for exceedingly long hours of work and risk-taking. Our government has traditionally achieved some success in establishing

anti-monopoly laws. We also have a graduated income tax system. Keep in mind, no system is perfect. However, ours has done
a fantastic job of stimulating creativity and lifting all boats in the
process.

The other crazy thing about the free enterprise system is how
it causes people to innately serve one another. We do not con-
sistently serve others just because we feel like it. People usually
find jobs or start businesses and work because they need money
to buy necessities and have some freedom. Work appears, on the
surface, a selfish motive, and may actually be so for some people. In reality, anyone who works is serving others. A person's
labor or service is valuable to others, or the person does not get
paid. This is why the air-conditioning guy shows up when the
outside temperature is 98° and goes into your sweltering attic to
fix your air conditioner. When he finishes, you thank him like he
is a Superhero, and write him a check. You are happy, and he is
happy. Multiply similar services hundreds of thousands of times
amongst a myriad of different businesses and professions and
you have our country—when it is working properly.

A GOVERNMENT THAT GUARANTEES FREEDOM

Our form of government is the second necessary component of
a system that works in the real world. Since 1789, the average
lifespan of various country's constitutions across the globe is
approximately 17 years.[12] The United States Constitution is now
233 years old. The original framers must have gotten something
right. But what? One of the first things they got right derives
from the belief that people are created equal, concerning rights,
and at the same time, are imperfect. King George III put his pants

on one leg at a time, just like us; and he was flawed, just like us. Flawed, imperfect people should not have absolute power over others. The founders committed to having three equal branches of government that would each check the power of the other branches. These are, of course, the legislative branch, the executive branch, and the judicial branch. There was no allowance for a King of the United States since power corrupts, and absolute power corrupts absolutely. Also, the federal government was only to have the powers specified in the Constitution. The Bill of Rights protected the citizens, and the federal government was restrained in power so they could not take those rights away.

This democratic republic form of government works in the real world because it accounts for how people really behave. There is no utopian ideal suggesting the federal government should have massive power because they are angels. They are not angels and never will be. We must watch them incessantly and vote out of office anyone who neglects to fulfill the will of the electorate.

People may think they want the government to take care of them, but this is a bad bargain. They will mostly give you the impression of taking care of you as they steal more of your freedoms. As a nation, we can take care of ourselves better than the government can take care of us. Freedom, creativity, and productivity go hand in hand. The government makes for a miserable family. You never really want to invite them over for Thanksgiving. It would just be awkward.

Besides, do you want somebody to take care of you who cannot even balance their checkbook? If you or your business balanced the books the same way our federal government does, you would go to jail. We are not allowed to run Ponzi schemes or say there is money in places where there is none. The government's

Ponzi scheme is not much of a secret anymore. US citizens know that our government has saddled the younger generations with enormous debt. When an elected leader tries to address the debt problem, the media at large ignores them. I do not understand why this is the case. I hope a truly great generation will some-day hold our federal government accountable for their spending problem.

There are many good people in our federal, state, and local governments. They work hard and try to do what is right. There are also many things the government does that are positive and necessary. However, we need to vigilantly watch them and hold them accountable because they are imperfect, just like the rest of us.

VICTIM COLLECTORS

There is one last phenomenon we need to address concerning our present political landscape. It was alluded to in Chapter 1 in regards to your community leadership. If your leaders do not support (with both words and action) protecting the family, ad-vocating for work and local jobs creation, and treating others well, then they may not care about your success, no matter how much they say otherwise. In reality, they may actually be victim collectors.

Victim collectors are leaders who convince people in their community that they are victims and, thus, not responsible for their actions or own improvement. When people are fully con-vinced they are victims, they vote for that particular leader, and the leader "collects" them. The whole thing operates somewhat like a pyramid scheme. Leaders who collect the most victims voting for them receive the most power and highest salary as they move up from local to state levels and possibly on to the federal level. The whole thing is very insidious and hidden to the citizenry. The victim collecting world can include leaders from either political party, right or left. They never address or solve the actual problems but, instead, blame other groups.

Convincing people they are victims used to be somewhat tricky because people inherently want to solve their problems themselves. Personal responsibility allows one to fulfill the psychological need of competency, gives them a certain amount of control and freedom, and meets their need for purpose. However, with the constant bombardment of a message, even normal, competent people can come to believe they are victims. The greatest help in establishing victimhood is finding a group of people to target as the perpetrator of some injustice to vilify them. In pre-World War II Germany, the people were taught to vilify the Jews even though the Jewish people were a hard-working group just trying to provide for their own families and communities. In Russia and China, the Marxists always used the class warfare strategy to vilify people who may have owned a couple of cows or pigs or chickens more than the average person.

Victim collectors in our country will use class, race, or almost anything available to condemn a group if it meets their purposes. It is possible to target almost any group since there is no perfect group of people. There are always isolated incidences of injustice. The trick is to make a few incidents look like the whole group commits them or approves of them even though there may be little data to support the conclusion. If certain people play the message continuously, others start believing it. This never-ending message demonstrates the power of propaganda. The targeted group can be law-abiding, hard-working individuals just trying to make a living and take care of their families. In our country, we still have laws that make it illegal to punish people for crimes they did not do. So there may be hope, but I'm not sure. Propaganda is an exceptionally dangerous and powerful tool.

Obviously, not everyone is a victim collector. We have some current cultural circumstances, though, that make it easy to identify some victim collectors. The elephant in the living room causing massive community disintegration (that no one seems to want to talk about) is family breakdown. Honest social scientists can quickly tell you that communities with few fathers in the home become very unstable. This is not rocket science. American philosopher Allan Bloom already referred to it as the main problem in society 40 years ago.[13] When a father and a mother are both in a home raising, protecting, and caring for children, there are incredibly positive results for both the family and the outlying community. You can readily identify victim collectors as leaders who do not seem to care that there are no fathers in the homes. They may, surprisingly, advocate for and pass laws and policies that hurt the nuclear family. It is almost as if they know fatherless communities will eventually produce more victims who ultimately vote for them.

The next sure fired way of identifying a victim collector is truly eye-opening. One of the greatest needs in any community is good schools. Unfortunately, we have many areas in our country that have failing school systems. The parents in these communities desperately want their children to go to a first-rate school. They will do almost anything to get their kids into a capable school. They would love to have some kind of choice of school for their children to attend. However, a victim collector will not allow any type of school choice, and here is the part that is telling. The victim collector sends their children to a private school because they have the means to do so, but the people under them have to send their children to failing schools. They tell the people under them that school vouchers are bad. They have repeated the message so often that people will hear the word "voucher" and immediately associate something terrible with it. It would not matter if they used school "coupons" as the mechanism to designate your tax dollars to the school of your choice. They would just bombard people with "coupons are bad." It is the same if you called it a freedom card that allowed you to choose a school; then, somehow, "freedom cards" would also be horrible. This whole time, the victim collector is sending their kids to a private school or a good school in a different neighborhood. It is almost like they know failing schools produce more victims and give them more power. How can this happen?

Well, one way this can happen is because victim collectors always have helpers that benefit from the whole gambit. The local school administrator may have gained advancement to their position by the victim collector and his allies. The victim collector receives, in turn, large campaign contributions from teacher's unions or lobbying groups. They may all agree philosophically and will allow nothing to get in the way of the public school monopoly. If parents could choose a school that taught solid academics as well as moral ethics, character development, civic duty, and individual responsibility, the parents would pick that school. The graduates could become responsible citizens who can think for themselves and value family, hard work and treating others well. However, this would easily dismantle the belief in victimhood. People like this are an enormous threat to the victim collecting world.

Victim collectors always have helpers all up and down the chain who gain either monetarily or philosophically by perpetuating the entire system. Some American universities produce graduates who practically have degrees in victimhood. Frequently, victim collectors get kickbacks or campaign contributions from their helpers. There is a lot of money to spread around. The United States has spent $22 trillion on the war on poverty since 1964, and we have the same percentage of people in poverty as we had then. If you were to divide that $22 trillion up among 20 million families of four and gave it to them directly, each family would have received $1.1 million. We know the individual families did not receive all that money, but the helpers undoubtedly received much more than their fair share.

Most recently, victim collectors exposed themselves by the subtle, and not-so-subtle, encouragement of rioting, looting, and burning in many neighborhoods. They have given their support to groups that advocate anarchy, Marxism, and the destruction of the nuclear family. They have stood by and witnessed the destruction while saying very little or even giving support. They join in calling for the defunding of the police, a group approved of by a vast majority of Americans. Senior victim collectors have private bodyguards funded by taxpayers, so they are not overly concerned with an increase in crime. The victim collectors and their helpers also know the police in their own neighborhoods are well funded.

The older residents and local business owners in the destroyed neighborhoods realize that when the television cameras leave, they will live amongst graffiti-laden plywood, broken windows, and vacant buildings. Businesses shut down or move away, destroying numerous jobs. The remaining residents will struggle to find a pharmacy or grocery store nearby because they are all closed. Crime will increase dramatically because the police are defunded and have low morale. The victim collectors

are not disturbed by this because they live in safer neighborhoods, even gated communities, immune to the destruction. The
cherished result for them is that certain groups are vilified, and
Americans are divided. They know the burned-out neighborhoods have the potential of producing many more victims that
will someday give them even more power.

Victim collectors and their helpers always focus on obscure
problems that are irrelevant to the real issues in struggling neighborhoods. As with fatherlessness, failing schools, and boarded-
up businesses, they are not concerned with the opiate and drug
epidemic. They are far more likely to be consumed with which
bathroom people can use. They are like the photographer taking
a photo of small children. The kids look like they want to cry,
so the photographer holds up a puppet or other distractions to
divert their attention. Victim collectors always want us to focus
on something obscure because if you looked at them and what
they are really doing, you would want to scream.

We have a lot of communities that are truly in need. There
are real heroes in these neighborhoods—people who volunteer
their time and resources, building the values that lead to healthy
families. They model a high work ethic and treating others well,
and fiercely fight for the ability to choose a competent school.
They instinctively know that protecting people from all the risks
and consequences in their lives actually enslaves them in a form
of dependence. It takes away the incentive and motivation to
work, sacrifice, and overcome obstacles—the traits that lead to
success.

Victimhood is toxic, even corrosive to the soul. It freezes a
person in anger as they learn to hate some outside group. Angry
people have great difficulty treating others the way they would
like to be treated themselves. The next great generation will

reject the failed message of the victim collectors and their helpers and learn to help people responsibly.

The tone in this chapter is more direct and emphatic. The reason for this is because the stakes are so high. When nations have immersed themselves in socialism or vilifying other groups, the outcomes have been disastrous, and there is no easy reversal. However, we still need to be able to discuss our government with one another reasonably and intelligently. It is helpful to acknowledge that both sides usually want to help people. Therefore, we can respect one another's opinions and learn from others who have different views than us. It is OK to disagree. We can learn a great deal from people who disagree with us. The best ideas have a chance when expressed within the context of civil and open debate.

5

HIGHER EDUCATION
The Truth About Words

IN ALLAN BLOOM'S BESTSELLING BOOK, *The Closing of the American Mind*, already in 1987, he writes,

> There is one thing a professor can be absolutely certain of: almost every student entering the University believes, or says he believes, that truth is relative...The students' backgrounds are as various as America can provide. Some are religious, some are atheists; some are to the Left, some to the Right; some intend to be scientists, some humanists or professionals or businessmen; some are poor, some rich. They are unified only in their relativism....[1]

Who can blame them? If I were 18 and on my own for the first time, this is exactly what I would want to believe. I would have latched on to this mantra and sat lovingly at the feet of anyone who proclaimed it. Any professor espousing this is immediately as popular as a rock star. Bring on massive beer, sex, drugs, whatever! Because we all know if your truth is your truth and my truth is my truth, then you can pretty much do anything you want, as long as it does not hurt anybody else, of course.

Much has been written about postmodernism. The postmodernist believes truth is relative and everything is open to interpretation. The definition of the philosophy shifts somewhat from source to source highlighting the difficulty of defining a belief system if you don't believe in truth. Some think this ideology is already on the way out. I wish I did not have to devote an entire chapter to such a common-sense issue, but for obvious reasons, relativism seems to die a slow death. Truth is critically important to everything we have said and what we are going to say. Unless we discuss the topic now, there is no reason to continue with the book, or as you will see, any book, for that matter. If truth is relative, then learning is either impossible or useless or both. Why would anybody pay colossal amounts of money for a college education if the professors do not have the truth to teach you? If you were taught similar ideas in college, you need to go back and demand a refund.

ASTOUNDING CONTRADICTIONS

What no one seems to notice or talk about is that every person who argues there is no truth uses words to make their case. So what exactly is a word? It is not the kind of thing we discuss at lunch while out with our friends. A *word* is a unit of language that has meaning. Meaning exists if it conveys something accurately or truthfully. Words are literally, then, truth dependent vehicles and, ultimately, the bearers of thought.[2] I know this is a mouthful, but we have to really get back to basics to see what is going on.

We have people arguing that there is no truth (or that truth is all relative), while they are using words that are truth dependent to make their case. This scenario is comparable to someone entering a classroom and stating to everyone that they would give anything if they could speak a word of English. If they could just speak one word of English, their happiness would never cease; all while they are speaking English.

This is the kind of stuff that makes our head hurt. The reason deep down we are so bothered is that we know it is totally contradictory. In fact, it violates what is known as the *law of non-contradiction*. The law of non-contradiction says that something cannot be both true and false at the same time and in the same sense. Anything that violates this law is unsupported and falls apart logically into thin air.[3] The law of non-contradiction is probably the most important law of all of logic; and if it is ignored or violated, philosophers would say all learning is impossible. If a postmodernist tries to argue with you about truth, you can remind them that their argument is meaningless unless their words have truth. When they say you are just using truth and rationality to enslave the world, you can ask them if they want you to respond with an irrational or rational answer. They only want their version of rationality to be allowed. The hypocrisy is almost amusing.

When we use words with other descriptive words and with the proper grammar, we can narrowly describe time, people, places, and things in a very truthful way if we so desire. We can also lie, but that says nothing about words having accurate, truthful, characteristics and everything about someone having lying thoughts. The words are simply bearers of that thought. If words weren't truth dependent, then we would not be guilty of lying or possibly a lot of other things. Maybe that was the goal all along.

Another more common method of pointing out the contradiction of relative truth is by simply showing that the statement, "There is no truth," is a truth statement itself. You are saying there is no truth as you make a truth statement. This is similar to our previous example, except when the person enters the classroom, they say, "There is no such thing as the English language. The English language does not exist and was never invented or ever spoken." They say this while they are speaking the English language. The logic just falls apart on so many levels. The Emperor has no clothes.

GROUPTHINK

The story by Hans Christian Anderson is about an Emperor who cares nothing about running the country and only cares about his wardrobe. Two swindlers come into town, promising to weave the most amazing set of clothes ever. The Emperor decides he must have them. Anyone who does not agree that they are the most exquisite ever produced is a fool and not fit for their position. The swindlers pretend to make clothes on their loom, and no one dares to state the obvious for fear of being ostracized. Even the Emperor is afraid to say the invisible clothes do not exist and pretends to put them on and commences to walk around the kingdom in a procession. No one will state the glaring truth. Finally, a child blurts out, "The Emperor has no clothes!" All the people finally repeat it among themselves. Interestingly, even though the Emperor shivers from the chill and suspects the people are right, he never acknowledges the truth, and the procession continues.

And so the procession continues in academia. The professors are unwilling to state the obvious, probably out of fear of going against the crowd. Never underestimate the power of groupthink, especially if it could affect one's income. People become severely myopic when competing ideas are not allowed. Fortunately, relativism falls apart in the real world, as so many things do. It is like someone pulled over for speeding in a 35 mile-per-hour zone. They tell the police officer they weren't speeding because they always read the five before the three. Their truth says the speed limit is actually 53 mph. A several hundred dollar fine is the only thing that can quickly bring them back to reality. Well, maybe one more thing. Tell the professor you intensely dislike red cars and then spray-paint his new red Tesla with green and white stripes. All of a sudden, the professor is no longer a relativist.

CAN WE DEFINE TRUTH?

The fact is people who say there is no truth demand truth in every aspect of their lives. The relativist even demands truth in their relationships. I am pretty sure they would not act amused if their spouse used relative truth within the context of fidelity. They demand truth from their doctor (and the validity of the medical school degree hanging on their wall), their banker, restaurants, dry cleaners, military, police, airlines, manufacturers, organic farmers, and other businesses and services.[4] If these things were run in a relativistic way, society would be a mess. You can unequivocally say truth feeds and clothes the poor and makes nations wealthy and safe.[5]

Truth is also easily defined. Truth is that which describes an actual state of affairs, or telling it like it is, or that which corresponds to its object. Truth also has six characteristics that spell the acronym

ADVENT. I am not trying to make a theological statement; it is just the only acronym that works to remember these characteristics. All truth is (A) Absolute, even when it appears relative. If I say I was warm yesterday, that seems to be a relative truth. However, if I was in Phoenix and running to the top of Camelback Mountain when the temperature was 101°, I can assure you I was warm. All truth is (D) Discovered, not invented. Isaac Newton discovered the laws of gravity and motion; he did not make them up. All truth is (V) Very, very unchanging. Our ideas about truth change, but truth itself does not. Some people may have thought the earth flat at one time, but that did not change the fact that our planet has always been a sphere. All truth is (E) Exclusive; it excludes its opposite. Truth is (N) Narrowly defined, knowable, and supported by the facts and evidence. Lastly, all truth is (T) Transcultural.[6] Years ago, the house we lived in had a chain-link fence (because my wife wanted it). I put that fence in myself with great pain and effort—I suffered a smashed thumb while hammering in the posts. Anyway, the fact that I had a chain-link fence was true and could be described to any other culture. I just may have had to use a different language, or even pictures, to describe it.

I know this list is rather extensive and not what we pull out to use in normal conversation. However, it is beneficial and necessary in guiding our thoughts and beliefs so as not to get swept away by someone else's ill-grounded philosophy. As professor and writer C. S. Lewis said, "Good philosophy must exist, if for no other reason because bad philosophy needs to be answered."[7]

TRUTH AND MORALITY

At this juncture, a postmodern may contend that they only believe there is no absolute truth in regards to morality. A good question to ask in return is whether or not they believe in having laws. Should we have laws? The normal response is that, of course, we have to have laws or society breaks down. So here is the critical point. A law determines one thing right and another thing wrong. Morality also determines one thing right and another thing wrong. It turns out all laws legislate morality; it is just a matter of whose morality you are going to legislate.[8]

Since we have determined that some laws are good to have and others are not so good (i.e., some countries still cut off the hand of a thief), then it also bears out that there is truth in some moral codes being bad for a society and others that are good for society. We can then start having the conversation concerning our legal code, knowing that there is truth in morality and also truth concerning which laws are best. For instance, we can acknowledge the truth that certain behaviors are bad for the person committing them, bad for us, and bad for our children if it is not even safe for them to go outside or venture into nearby areas. Once that truth is established, communities can devise laws limiting dangerous and bad behavior to protect families and children. We can all agree that a people who police themselves to the max extent possible, guided by a high moral code, is the best situation because it requires the least amount of legal enforcement. If we destroy truth, then we also destroy morality, our laws, and eventually our communities—truth matters.

TRUTH AND METANARRATIVE

Now the postmodern may finally say that he or she actually believes there is no absolute truth regarding any grand metanarrative or overall set of values and beliefs. They might say no comprehensive viewpoint is better than another; it is all in the eye of the beholder. The Nazis facing prosecution for their crimes at the Nuremberg war trial would have loved this idea. They could have simply stated, "Who are you to judge what we felt was right? We were only doing what was morally correct for us as a culture and following our superiors' orders." What does the postmodern say to them? The same could be said about headhunting and cannibalistic cultures throughout the primitive world. You are forced to ask the relativist, "In some cultures they love their neighbors; in other cultures they eat them. Do you have a personal preference, and if so, what is it?"[9] Societies follow a set of values and beliefs that lead to their actions. The truth is some of these values and beliefs are better than others.

Most religions and belief systems also make exclusive truth claims, and many of these truth claims can be evaluated on scientific evidence and historical facts. It is possible to make judgments on metanarratives based on this realization. We already know that mutually exclusive truth claims cannot both be true. If one belief system states as fact something that is totally contradictory to another religion or belief system, then they cannot both be true. Remember, if you violate the law of non-contradiction, then nothing is knowable. Postmodernism seems to lead to what we call pluralism, which believes that all religions or worldviews are ultimately true. The rest of the world does not believe this at all. They know their belief systems make exclusive truth claims, and therefore, this is utterly impossible. The relativism of pluralism appears so tolerant and accepting until you ask them if they are forcing relativism on you. Who dictated pluralism when we know it violates all logic? Therefore, relativism or pluralism is just as exclusive as any other belief system.

Relativism also has a toxic effect on a person's view of purpose in life. The unrelenting pursuit of truth has historically been considered one of life's great purposes. People were serious about education, both formally and informally, for this reason. An educated person was considered someone who could think critically in diverse fields. Under this definition, someone with a PhD may not be considered very educated if he knows nothing outside his very narrow field. Many professors do have a diverse educational background and are very hard-working and good people. I owe a lot to those who poured into me. Not all of them are necessarily well-read in broad subject areas and may never have held a job outside academia. Perhaps this narrow focus has led them to a distorted view of truth and, ultimately, to nihilism, the rejection of all religious and moral principles in the belief that life is meaningless. Before the 1960s, teenage suicide was virtually nonexistent among American youth. By 1980, 400,000 teens attempted it every year.[10] The suicide rate among people 10-24 years old increased by 56% from 2007 to 2017 and is now the second leading cause of death in this age group.[11] I don't think these statistics are an unexplained accident. Nihilism leads to pessimistic gloom and severe depression.

THE ORIGINS OF POSTMODERNISM

Postmodernism, or relativism, is so ludicrous and easily discredited you eventually wonder who brought this stuff into our culture. We can trace much of it to critical theory that came out of the Frankfurt School in the 1930s. This was the first Marxist-oriented research center affiliated with a major German university. Max Harkheimer, an early leader of the school, believed the West represented inequality, domination, and exploitation. Consequently, he led his associated thinkers on a full-scale war with Western civilization. The later forbearers of postmodernism, Jacques Derrida and Michael Foucault, can still trace their deconstructionist mindset (deconstructing any creative work according to the whims of the existing cultural or individual mindset) back to the Frankfurt School.[12] Since truth and rationality make up a major part of Western civilization's foundation, then we can deduce that postmodernism is an outright attack on life as we know it in the West and, therefore, achieves a major goal of the Marxist based Frankfurt School.

Public universities who advocate postmodernism are directly attacking our country, democracy, and the free enterprise system that has given us massive benefits and our way of life the last several hundred years; and that attack is funded by our tax dollars. Wow, we are paying for our own demise!

The fact that many universities attack Western civilization is well-documented to the point that I do not think anyone even disputes it anymore.[13] The answer as to why they do is probably varied and complex. Perhaps they believe in utopian systems that are not compatible with our form of government and a free enterprise system. Whatever the reason, it appears they have found a way to attack everything our country represents. The results of the attack are devastating both on a personal level, and for the nation as a whole.

OUR MOST IMPORTANT CHOICES

When you ask young people today what their most important choices will be, they usually answer with something like where they will live, what career they will go into, what future school they will attend, or who their future spouse will be. These are all significant decisions, but in reality, the most important choices people make are their moral choices. The moral choices we make will affect us physically, financially, and socially (i.e., health, wealth, family, and friends), more than any other choice.[14] For instance, if someone decides to use meth, they can quickly end up addicted. The meth will eventually destroy their teeth, damage several organs, cause facial sores, damage their nasal passages, and cause sleeplessness and severe weight loss. In the process, they find it difficult to hold down a job, and their finances suffer. They also may find they do not have the friends they once had, or worse, observe the destruction of their family. Other types of drugs and alcohol can damage the body as well. People with incredible talent, such as actors and professional athletes, have destroyed their lives with drugs and alcohol. News sources have chronicled so many of these that there is really no need to mention specific examples.

People who have an excellent education, career, and marry well can also destroy their lives through their moral choices. In 2001 the leaders of Enron Corporation appeared outwardly very successful. Unfortunately, Ken Lay, Jeff Skilling, and Andy Fastow were cooking the books and were sentenced to prison for conspiracy, insider trading, making false statements to prosecutors, and securities fraud. The next year Bernie Ebbers was convicted of similar crimes as he led WorldCom. A few years later, Bernie Madoff, who once ran the NASDAQ, was convicted of running the largest Ponzi scheme in the history of the world. Many honest, hard-working people lost their life-savings due to their crimes. Lest we forget, there are the Harvey Weinsteins out there to remind us what a lack of morality in sexual ethics can do to a person. All of these men had good educations and, yet, destroyed their lives (and the lives of others) financially, socially, and sometimes physically by their moral choices. I could go on, but I think you get the idea.

To connect the dots of some of the things we have discussed, let us review. As we have seen, if you destroy truth, you destroy morality. If truth is relative, then so is morality. But, as we have seen, the most important decisions a person can make are their moral choices. The younger generations are set up for failure when they are not taught and alerted to the incredible dangers of making immoral decisions. The most important task of a civilization is the upbringing of its children. If these children are led astray, they will lead unproductive lives and produce dysfunctional families, which eventually destroys society as we know it. So, when postmodernism destroys truth, it destroys morality, which destroys the ability of a generation to make their most important choices, destroying the family, and thus a civilization. I consider this a fairly important thing to ponder.

Education that is not anchored in truth and morality can lead to extremely detrimental outcomes. Haim G. Ginott was an educator and a survivor of a Nazi concentration camp. He stated that he is suspicious of education:

> I am a survivor of a concentration camp. My eyes saw what no man should witness: gas chambers built by learned engineers, children poisoned by educated physicians, infants killed by trained nurses, women and babies shot and burned by high school and college graduates. So I am suspicious of education. My request is: help your students become human. Your efforts must never produce learned monsters, skilled psychopaths, educated Eichmanns. Reading, writing, arithmetic are important only if they serve to make our children more human.[15]

We should always be suspicious of education based on a dangerously deficient view of morality.

Some of the oldest of the Millennials are getting ready to send their children out into the world. Another generation will enroll in technical schools, go directly into the workforce, enter the military, or perhaps pursue higher education. The question is, will they have a foundation for making good moral decisions, or will they follow instinct, peer pressure, or the flowery sounding nihilistic teachings of a professor or teacher who holds the reins of power over their grade. They may come back home at Christmas and enlighten poor mom and dad about the shortcomings of their old-fashioned beliefs. They may dismiss or argue against your appeals to experience, history, and logic using the most current social media sound bites. They may say your truth is your truth, and their truth is their truth. As they continue to argue to make their case, you may want to remind them that you notice that they are using words.

6

SCIENCE

25 Years of Surprises

STUFF WEARS OUT. THE LONGER I live on the planet, the more I am forced to deal with this reality. I seem to spend more of my free time than I would like fixing cars, sanding and painting window sills, replacing broken appliances, repairing rotten landscape timbers, and the list goes on. This breaking down of things is due to the second law of thermodynamics, which says everything tends towards a lower energy state or greater randomness (greater entropy). As far as we know, this is true in the entire universe. Everything eventually wears out and turns to dust—but then, you get up and look out the window and see complexity, some order, and new things sprouting up. Obviously, those things that are powered by a digital base-4 information processing system seem to overcome the second law, not individually, but as a species. The response to what I have just said will be, for the vast majority of people, "Huh?" Hardly anyone talks about this, and yet, it is true. Please bear with me. I have used some terms that people frequently use in our modern age; however, most of us do not fully understand what they mean. I will try to explain what scientists are discovering in the field of biology by breaking down these terms in, hopefully, an easy to understand and lighthearted way. In doing so, my desire is for the reader to comprehend more of the world around them and retain it because this knowledge has enormous implications regarding our worldview.

The first word I used in the clause above that is difficult to comprehend is digital. We live in the digital age and everything is digital this and digital that. We know that digital has something to do with numbers, but it must mean more than that because humanity has used numbers for thousands of years. Yet the digital age infancy began only about 70 years ago. We need a good fictional story to help us understand some things, or this could get boring.

SUSPENSE OVER SCHWEINFURT

The setting is England, early October 1943. The extremely attractive and well educated, 21-year-old Victoria Kensington is the secretary and personal assistant to Air Commodore Jack Harris at Bomber Command Headquarters, RAF High Wycombe, just northwest of London. What no one around her knows is that Ms. Kensington is also a German spy. Her parents were born in Berlin and partly educated in England. After World War I, the Weimar Republic government recruited them to move to England with fabricated identification. Victoria was born near London in 1922. The Kensingtons mixed easily within British society, and their only daughter attended some of the best schools in London. She is fiercely loyal to her parents and their homeland. She is also currently the most highly valued asset in all of German military intelligence.

The British and American Allied Air Forces have just initiated a new strategy of precision daylight bombing campaigns deep within Germany. Though the Allied losses are heavy, they are still having a devastating effect on German strategic industrial output. The Nazis are doing everything in their power to find out in advance the exact time and target of the Allied bombing raids. There are eight critical target areas the Germans need to protect at all costs. They are consumed with finding out the exact time the bombers will arrive over these crucial cities or regions.

Ms. Kensington's exceptional good looks and charm make it easy for her to date several different RAF and American pilots in and around London. This combined with her access to information at Bomber Command headquarters, allows her to figure out the exact time and place of some of the Allies' largest bombing missions. There is one problem. Because of her high value, Victoria cannot exchange information directly with any other agent for fear the British will discover her true identity.

Mr. Robert Cole is the only agent allowed to have any kind of contact with Ms. Kensington. Like Victoria, Mr. Cole was also born in England to German transplants with altered identities. He is highly trained in a variety of skills and has secured a flat just 100 yards down and across the street from Ms. Kensington's apartment. Using his binoculars, he can look through a window to see the doorway of her bathroom. He is feverishly trying to figure out how she can relay a code to him without using anything conspicuous. At first he wonders if she could use the numbers on a bathroom scale or a barometer; but there is no way to see that kind of detail, especially in inclement weather. He determines that he might be able to see through her bathroom door opening three lights above her sink. However, the angle is such that he is reasonably sure he could not see more than three lights. He considers three regular white lights. Perhaps, Victoria could unscrew particular bulbs to form a code as in the first two bulbs out and the last one on, or the first one on and the last two off, and so forth. If there are only two possibilities, off and on, and three different lights, the number of possible combinations is 2x2x2 (2^3), which is only eight possibilities. She could relay to him eight different cities but not the eight different potential hours of the day. Because of their distance to the target and the length of the day available, the bombers usually strike between 9 AM and 4 PM. German high command wants to know which of eight possible targets and the nearest hour to enable Luftwaffe fighter squadrons to attack the bombers without running out of gas while loitering too long over the ambush point.

Then Mr. Cole has a revelation. If he installed three lights above her sink with a globe over each light and four different colors of movable glass inside each globe, then she could select four different colors on each light. Because there are 4 possibilities of color (not just on and off) and 3 different lights, the equation is 4x4x4 (4^3), which gives 64 possibilities. She can transmit to him one of eight different cities and one of eight possible hours of the day!

A few days later, Mr. Cole, disguised as a maintenance man, enters Ms. Kensington's apartment and installs three custom globed vanity lights above her sink. On the inside of each globe is hidden slidable glass that can cover the forward opening to give four different colors. The four possible colors are Amber, Cherry red, Turquoise blue, and Green. If anyone asks, they are just mood lights given to her as a gift. The two of them establish a time of 9:10 PM every evening for Mr. Cole to look through his binoculars. If there is a known target and time, she will set the proper color code and then open the door just long enough for him to see the three lights and their individual color.

Six days later, Mr. Cole is looking through his binoculars on a cold and rainy mid-October evening, wondering if again there would be no opening of the door. But this evening is different. Ms. Kensington has discovered that the next day an enormous bombing mission is planned on the ball-bearing factories in Schweinfurt at approximately 3 PM. She pulls out a hidden chart and transcribes Schweinfurt at 3 PM as GGA. At 9 PM, she raises the shade of her window and goes into her bathroom and closes the door. Victoria then arranges the three globes so that they illuminate Green, Green, and Amber. At precisely 9:10 PM, she opens her bathroom door and steps away for about 15 seconds. Just then, Mr. Cole excitedly writes down GGA from the green, green, and amber lights that he sees through his binoculars and looks again to make sure he observes correctly. Just that quickly, the door is closed. No one would have ever noticed what just took place, which is just as well for the two of them, or they would be executed. Now, he is all business as he calmly walks to a hidden radio and transmits on a predetermined frequency "Golf, Golf, Alpha," which is the phonetic alphabet for GGA. They cannot take a chance that anyone ever associates the colors of her vanity lights with the coded transmission. He says it again until he hears a distant but distinct, "Roger, Golf, Golf, Alpha."

German intelligence then translates the GGA from their code table of 64 possibilities as Schweinfurt at 3 PM and tells the German high command. Almost immediately, large numbers of German anti-aircraft artillery (dreaded 88mm "flak" guns) are scheduled to reposition on railroad cars, and numerous Luftwaffe fighter squadrons are given orders to fly the next day to airfields near Schweinfurt or near the likely route the bombers will take.

	9am	10am	11am	12am	1pm	2pm	3pm	4pm
Frank-furt	TTT	TCT	TAT	TGT	ATT	ACT	AGT	AAT
Col-ogn	TTC	TCC	TAC	TGC	ATC	ACC	AGC	AAC
Dres-den	TTA	TCA	TAA	TGA	ATA	ACA	AGA	AAA
Dort-mund	TTG	TCG	TAG	TGG	ATG	ACG	AGG	AAG
Duss-el-dorf	CTT	CCT	CAT	CGT	GTT	GCT	GGT	GAT
Essen	CTC	CCC	CAC	CGC	GTC	GCC	GGC	GAC
Schw-ein-furt	CTA	CCA	CAA	CGA	GTA	GCA	GGA	GAA
Stutt-gart	CTG	CCG	CAG	CGG	GTG	GCG	GGG	GAG

It is amazing that a simple three-letter code, when transcribed correctly, sent, and then translated on the other end, could reposition a large part of Germany's air defense forces. Information is very powerful. The second gigantic bombing mission over Schweinfurt (the first mission was August 17) actually did take place the afternoon of 14 October, 1943. Thankfully, the rest of the above story is fictional because Allied bomber losses were already terrible. The courage of those young flyers was unbelievable, and we owe our liberty to sacrifice like theirs.

THE DIGITAL WORLD

If you were able to track with the previous story and understand Victoria's vanity lights, then you are well on your way to understanding the digital world and some fundamentals of microbiology. When Mr. Cole was contemplating using three normal lights with the option of each light being either on or off, he played with the idea of using a digital base-2 code. Digital does, in fact, have something to do with numbers, but it is only the number of possible outcomes at each position. Ordinary white lights that are either on or off represent two options and, thus, digital base-2. As we saw, that could generate only eight possible outcomes from the three lights (2x2x2) and, therefore, could not convey enough information.

We usually do not think much about what information means because we inherently know it informs; but information also excludes possibilities. With only eight different on/off options available from the three lights, not enough variables could be excluded. They could convey the city target but not the time. German high command needed to know the precise target and exact time. It is a little like asking your friend if Emily is going to have a party at her house this weekend, and your friend responds that she is going to have a party and not going to have a party. This tells you nothing. She has to exclude one or the other to provide you with the requested information.

When Mr. Cole had the idea to use four different color lights at each of the three positions, he converted to digital base-4. The base-4 simply represents four different possible outcomes at each light position. The formula for the potential amount of information carried is always the number of possibilities multiplied sequentially by the number of lights (code positions), which is 4x4x4 (4^3) and gives 64 possible outcomes. With that amount of information-carrying capacity, they could exclude all the other possibilities so as to convey time and place with the three selected colors. Now, we can make some interesting comparisons.

We, the human race, mostly only use digital base-2 in our digital technology. Instead of lights, we use simple on-off switches on silicon chips. Computers read these as zero being off and one being on. It is still very much like the white vanity lights that are either on or off. If Mr. Cole had been able to see 6 vanity lights through the door opening, he could have used plain white lights because the formula of 2 possibilities multiplied by 6 lights is sequentially 2x2x2x2x2x2, or 2^6, which yields 64 options.

If he could have seen 8 different lights, then the information-carrying capacity would have been 2^8, which equals 256 possibilities. We use groups of eight positions in our digital world since base-2 is kind of weak. We call each on-off switch position a "bit" instead of a vanity light, and when we have eight of them together, we call it a byte. Therefore, if Victoria sat in front of eight ordinary white vanity lights (bits), getting ready for an evening out, she would represent one byte. If there were 1,024 people, each in front of an 8-light vanity (imagine different combinations of them being off or on), that would be a kilobyte, a little over 1 million is a megabyte, and a little over 1 billion is a gigabyte. Computers store large amounts of information with simple zeros and ones organized in bytes.

There is one more thing to consider. If we could use four

different voltages at each switch (or bit) position inside our computers, we could convert it to a digital base-4 just like each light having four different colors. Our computers would carry hundreds of times more information. Each eight-light vanity (byte) with four possible outcomes at each position would carry 4x4x4x4x4x4x4x4, or 4^8. That is 65,536 informational possibilities versus just 256 for base-2. You can see digital base-4 is far more powerful than base-2. I find it fascinating that we are only advanced enough to use a digital base-2 system in our devices after centuries of human technological progress, but living things use digital base-4.

There are just a couple of more items we have to cover to better understand our digital world. In the earlier story, I said Mr. Cole initially thought of viewing the numbers on an old-fashioned scale that you can measure weights on by sliding weights on a kind of pendulum arm, like at the doctor's office, or he was possibly thinking of a barometer. I included these because they are good examples of the analog technology that came before the digital age. Analog devices measure some physical phenomenon directly and uses a mechanical system, fluid, air pressure, or some other measurable input to give a readable numeric value. The old-fashioned Mercury thermometer is also an excellent example of an analog device.

Digital systems are different and much more complicated. Let me explain. When Victoria found out the next day's target was Schweinfurt at 3 PM, she had to transcribe that information into a code (GGA) and then transmit it to Mr. Cole, who merely passed it on to German intelligence. German intelligence translated GGA back into usable information, which was Schweinfurt at 3 PM. Victoria's mind provided the processing power to transcribe it into the three-letter code. The information was then transmitted, and German intelligence provided the processing power on the other end to translate the code back into usable information. Computer science types might call this transcription processing and translation processing something different. I have used these terms for simplicity since they will relate to some of the upcoming examples. One can see that in digital devices, there is often a certain amount of processing of the information into a digital format, then the transmission of the digital code, and finally, the processing of the digital code back into information for display or use.

Lastly, you need an overall system to do something constructive (or, in this case, destructive) with the final transmitted information. The German high command was the system that used the information to reposition a large part of the German air defense forces.

Now you should finally have a grasp of the sentence that included the words "digital base-4," "information," "processing," and "system." I only have to apologize that you may never look at vanity lights the same ever again. Now, let us apply what we just learned to the realm of living things. A word of caution is in order, though. I have temporarily changed many of the terms scientists use to describe these essential components of life. A professional scientist would probably be offended and tell me I cannot do this. Well, I just did. I am kind of a rebel that way. I will do whatever it takes for people to comprehend somewhat difficult processes.

A CITY RUN BY ROBOTS

Cells are the basic structural unit of all living things. Some animal or plant life contains a single cell and others up to trillions of cells. Humans perhaps have close to 40 trillion cells in their body. If we were to magnify one of these cells millions of times, we could compare it to a space-age, futuristic city run by robots. I am not the first one to make this comparison. Biochemists use nuclear magnetic resonance and electron microscopes to observe life at the molecular level and see it almost as a series of snap-together beads. They have noticed the similarity to the advanced objects that we build.

In 3-D, we would see many of these robots flying all over the place doing the city's work and repair functions. These robots are also like really advanced machines and tools, the type you would buy at a futuristic hardware/electronics store. They are comparable to exceptional pumps, motors, saws, transporters, garbage collection and recycling machines, encoding and decoding machines, and more. In fact, they are so efficient and exceptional we will call them Pro-machines because they are truly professional level. Pro-machines are constructed from numerous combinations of Amazing Action parts. Amazing Action parts are like Lego® pieces prearranged to form 20 different patterns. The Pro-Machines are made from hundreds, or even thousands, of these same 20 different Amazing Action parts. Like all machines, they eventually wear out and have to be replaced. We will now examine the automatic process by which the cell replaces these biochemical machines.

Imagine you are reduced in size so that you can hitch a ride on an intracellular transporter. As you are riding along, you see a sizable spherical building in the very center of the city with many openings and a lot of security. The large spherical building is the nucleus and also the Central Data Storage Vault. The transporter Pro-machine you are riding on flies off in the direction of one of the Vault's openings. Not just anything is allowed to pass through the opening. Apparently, your transporter displays the proper ID because you are allowed to enter.

Once inside the spherical Central Data Storage Vault building, you see an astonishingly long helical staircase. You jump off the transporter and onto the stairs in the nick of time, just before the transporter heads off somewhere else. Once on the staircase, you start to notice just how unique it is. The stairway is divided right down the middle, and if half of a stair is Turquoise on one side, then it is Amber on the other or vice versa. Likewise, if the stair is Green on one side, then it is Cherry on the other or vice versa. All the way up as far as the eye can see, alternating in no particular order as far as you can tell, a little over 3 billion stairs are connected in the middle; and if A is on one side, it always connects to T, or if G is on one side, it always connects to C. You can think of it as the Christmas colors, Cherry and Green, always attached. Likewise, the IKEA® colors of Amber and Turquoise always attach to one another. As you climb the stairs, you occasionally come upon a damaged stair displaying color only on one side. A machine comes along and repairs it, apparently knowing that if it connected to C, it has to be a G or if the damaged stair connected to T, it has to be A. Another unique fact you notice is that every region of stairs has a particular marking or address.

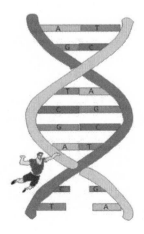

Fortunately, you have quick reflexes because as you continue to climb up the spiral staircase, the crazy thing splits apart right in your little region of stairs. You desperately hold on to the banister as you watch another exotic looking Pro-machine; actually an assemblage of combined machines, swoop in and start copying code in groups of three. Each group of three colors is called a codon. Each codon then is just like a three-letter word such as TTT, ATC, CAG, and so forth. The bizarre machine copies the exact colors from the split apart staircase except you can see that it substitutes Ultra-violet for the Turquoise. You notice the part of the machine touching three successive stairs (say a G, an A, and a T) on the staircase transcribed as GAU. You watch as it transcribes many of these groups of three (ATA, GCT, GGA, and on and on) from the split staircase, always substituting U for T.

Suddenly, the staircase comes back together. You hop on the Pro-machine as it flies off to another part of the ladder to extract some more groups of three-colored stairs, or codons. The machine seems to know the exact address it is going to as it moves along different parts of the ladder and extracts more codons. Finally, the assemblage of machines is filled with hundreds and hundreds of chemical codons; and it flies out to one of the openings going out of the Central Data Storage Vault, displays the proper ID, and is allowed to fly out to the area outside the nucleus.

One facet of the operation you are sure of now is that this Pro-machine knows its precise destination. It navigates along until it hooks up precisely with something called the Robots Home, a factory where they meticulously build robots. You watch as all the codons the Pro-machine is carrying are translated back to a code the factory understands. The factory knows how to process the information download accurately, excluding trillions of wrong ways the machine parts could have been assembled. Each three-color codon represents one of the 20 different Amazing Action parts, and factory robots insert the specific part on an assembly line in precise order. With every 3-letter codon representing one of the 20 different Amazing Action parts, the chain grows longer and longer until there are over 700 Amazing Action parts in exact order. It just so happens that the 20 different Amazing Action parts can come in a left-handed variety or a right-handed variety. However, the factory only uses the left-handed variety as it constructs the machine. Finally, at the very end, the three-letter codon UAG, instead of representing a specific Amazing Action part, signals the whole process to stop. The factory finally releases the Pro-machine, and other machines carefully fold it until it looks exactly like one of the machines you had noticed earlier that was wearing out.

WHAT IT ALL MEANS

What I have just described in plain English is what microbiologists and biochemists have known for some time. They merely use different terms rooted in Latin, Greek, or other languages. The Pro-machine is a protein. The 20 different types of Amazing Action parts used to construct the protein are amino acids. The initial Pro-machine transporter you hitched a ride on through the nuclear membrane was a protein transporter called Karyopherin (kind of sounds like "carry off the thing"). The spherical Central Data Storage Vault is the cell's nucleus, and the heavily guarded openings in the nucleus are called nuclear pores. The double-sided spiral staircase inside the nucleus is DNA. The side rails are made of sugar-phosphate molecules, and the stairs are made up of one of the four nucleotides A (adenine), C (cytosine), T (thymine), and G (guanine). Just remember the A and T always connect, and the C and G always connect.

The transcribing assemblage of Pro-machines that caused you to jump out of the way as it split the stairs apart is called, I am hesitant to say, RNA polymerase. No one I know remembers that word after about 10 seconds. It is easier to call it a transcribing assemblage. Anyway, this preprogrammed machine goes to addressed regions along the DNA chain. The region on the chain containing protein-coding instructions is called a gene (gene sounds a little like region if you drop the "re"). The transcribing assemblage (RNA polymerase) then transcribes the individual A, C, T and G's into triplets, or codons (AAG, CUG, ACU, on and on). Codon is kind of a cool word and one of the few I did not change since it describes, in a way, what is actually going on.

I used color association with the nitrogen bases (ACT and G), or stairs of the ladder, which does not necessarily carry over into the real world. However, it makes no difference to the preprogrammed transcribing machine whether it is a color, flavor, smell, or other chemical property. The vital concept to note is that there is an equal probability option of four different possibilities at each position on the chain, and the machine is programmed to distinguish them. These four different possibilities at each position on the DNA chain is what makes DNA a digital base-4 system. Just as Victoria used a preprogrammed chart to determine which color the three lights should be, the machine also knows how to copy the three nitrogen bases (stairs) off the ladder into a transportable code. I used the color scheme only because it transfers easily from our fictional story, and shows how the cell, at its most basic level, uses a digital base-4 system.

When the transcribing assemblage machine makes the

three-letter copy of each codon and uses ACU (uracil) and G, instead of ACT and G, then this becomes messenger RNA. The messenger RNA, while still in the nucleus, is worked on in an editing room called the spliceosome (think splice and edit) to make it perfect. The messenger RNA, consisting of hundreds of three-letter codons, finally leaves the nucleus and goes to the curious factory called the Robots Home. The scientific name for this factory is the ribosome. Again, it is a name that leaves us after about 10 seconds. I called it the Robots Home partly because it rhymes with the ribosome. The ribosomal factory has the necessary pre-programmed machines to translate the three-letter codons into the corresponding amino acid (Amazing Action part), insert the specific amino acid called for in the sequence, and start assembling them in perfect order on the factory assembly line. For instance, I just happened to have Victoria change the lights to GGA, which is also the codon for the amino acid lysine. When the factory receives GGA, it always places lysine at that position in the chain. Every three-letter code tells the factory to put one of the 20 specific amino acids (Amazing Action parts) at that particular place in the chain. The final product can have hundreds or even thousands of amino acids correctly sequenced. The final product is called a protein (Pro-machine).

This whole process is very similar to Victoria's transcribing the time and target to a three-letter code and displaying that code on her three multicolored vanity lights (her three vanity lights actually represent just one codon). Yet, the cell is transcribing millions, if not billions, of codons per second. Victoria then transmits the information. Mr. Cole receives it, changes the code slightly to a phonetic alphabet, and transmits it again to German military intelligence. Intelligence then translates the three-letter code into usable information for German high command. The cell's main difference is that everything is automatic and carried out very carefully by programmed machines.

The transcribing machine, just like Victoria, only needs 3 positions of code per codon because only 64 possibilities are required to represent each of the 20 different amino acids. It turns out DNA uses 60 of the possibilities to encode the 20 amino acids. There is redundancy since several different codons can represent the same amino acid. Scientists are not sure why yet. Also, one codon is used as a start command, and three of them are used as a stop command, which means the cell uses all 64 possible codon strings. Our discussion of the most basic part of the digital base-4 information processing system the cell uses is mostly complete. You now know more about protein synthesis than 99% of all people walking down the street. You may know more than you ever wanted, but at least now we can explore some fascinating things using this knowledge.

The first realization a person comes to is how complicated the process is. We have only recently uncovered just how finicky the ribosomal factory is in laying out all the amino acids to make a protein. There are only a limited number of ways to join them all together, or the whole thing unravels. Also, I mentioned earlier how the Amazing Action parts (amino acids) all have to be left-handed when used to make a protein. In nature, the amino acids are about equal numbers left-handed or right-handed (this left or right-handedness is called chirality). However, when the factory builds a Pro-machine or protein, every amino acid used is left-handed. A simple usable protein has about 150 amino acids (the number can go into the thousands for some proteins). Researchers have recently discovered that the odds of a simple protein coming together by chance is 1 in 1 x 10^{74}. I apologize for the heavy use of exponents but the scientific literature uses so many of them a person might have to use exponents to describe the number of times they use them. For the normal reader, exponents can be a breeze if you keep perspective by remembering a one in a million chance is 1 in 1 x 10^6 (sometimes shortened to just 10^{-6}). Also, mathematicians used to consider a probability of 1 in 1 x 10^{50} (10^{-50}) mathematically impossible. Probabilities beyond that are even more unlikely. With that in mind, there are approximately 1×10^{80} atoms in the universe. Only approximately 1×10^{40} proteins have ever existed on planet Earth. Comparing the numbers, one can safely say the odds of a protein forming by chance (10^{-74}) are unbelievably remote. It is also intriguing that the structures that hold DNA in place and the machines that read and manipulate the DNA are all proteins—but proteins are only made by fully functioning DNA. You get into a chicken or egg problem. Which came first, the chicken or the egg—the protein or the DNA?

CELLULAR COMPUTERS

Now is an excellent time to step back and take a look at the cell as a whole. One might wonder if there are just a couple of these protein factories, or ribosomes, in the cell. There are actually as many as 10 million ribosomes in a mammalian cell, and many of them may be specialized, each producing certain types of protein machines.[1] Each cell performs as many as one billion chemical reactions per second doing things like creating or using energy, manufacturing proteins for use inside and outside the cell, intercellular transportation, signaling, and making skin, bone, antibodies, hormones, and more.

The cell has to access the DNA continually for informational instruction to coordinate this mind-boggling workload. It is one thing to make all these proteins, and then it is another matter altogether to regulate the when, where, and how much. It appears protein machines are able to read the DNA in different ways to extract different information. They might even be able to read it not only forwards, but backwards. The cell can compact the spiral staircase DNA like a chain in a bucket. The DNA is compacted so tightly that the cell may actually read the information in ways we do not at all understand.

Not long ago, scientists thought 98% of the DNA in the cell was junk because they could only find about 2% that was encoding for specific proteins. This view is changing. Over the last decade, the Encyclopedia of DNA Elements (ENCODE) project, involving hundreds of scientists in laboratories worldwide, determined that at least 80% of DNA is biochemically active.[2] We just do not know exactly all the things it is doing. More than likely, a lot of those three billion A, C, T, and Gs are read by protein machines in unique ways to regulate cellular activity.

It is all working like a super-advanced computer system addressing and accessing the hard drive (DNA in the nucleus), making copies, and converting it to RAM (single-strand messenger RNA). The RAM info is then used by a CPU and 3-D printer (ribosome) to build the final product. The whole thing is completely automated and controlled by unfathomably complex micro machines receiving inputs somehow from the different ways the DNA is read. The central dogma of biology used to be DNA makes RNA which makes proteins, period. Now, there is more of a view towards a networking model, as in computer networks. In literature now published by the United States National Library of Medicine, you can find articles titled, "Will Biologists Become Computer Scientists?" The article concludes that "While cells and computers are made of very different materials—carbon versus silicone—both are nonetheless information-processing systems."[3] Bill Gates states, "DNA is like a computer program but far, far more advanced than any software we have ever created."[4]

The computer program part of this brings us back to where we started in this chapter. When we look at the world around us, we see everything breaking down and wearing out. The only things that overcome this are those powered by a digital base-4 information processing system. Every living thing has DNA and meets these criteria. They overcome entropy for great lengths of time as a species, but not individually. Life perpetuates itself because it is powered and controlled at the cellular level by a type of computer operating system far superior to anything humans can even dream of at this point in our technological progress. Man cannot build self-sufficient things, given only sunlight, water, air, and some nutrients. Consider how long it will be before we can construct a robot that repairs itself, regulates all its processes, and reproduces itself given only the basics for life. Our digital base-2 computer system and overall knowledge are woefully inadequate.

It should not surprise us that life needs the massively more powerful digital base-4 system to convert all the data into functional information that builds and controls micromachines. However, most people never saw this coming 25 years ago. It is, therefore, one of the greatest surprises in science over the last two decades. Every time we look under the hood of these micromachines with greater and greater detail, we keep finding greater and greater complexity. Dr. Francis Collins, who led the government side of mapping out the human genome (an organism's complete set of DNA), stated that even though they have mapped out the human genome, it will take decades, if not centuries, to understand its instructions.[5] It seems every year I am amazed by the new discoveries in microbiology; but this has not been the only surprise. The next one has to do with what we have learned about the universe.

EINSTEIN'S BLUNDER

If you go back 110 years to the early 1900s, scientists believed the universe was static and eternal. If someone believed back then that the universe had a beginning, the truly learned would view them with a certain amount of intellectual contempt. If they would not say it, they would at least think, "You poor, stupid person. You actually believe the universe had a beginning? Scientists know that it has always been static and eternal." With that as a backdrop, we can understand why Albert Einstein thought the same thing. In 1915, his theory of general relativity demonstrated that gravity could be explained as mass bending the space-time fabric. Time, space, and matter are all correlative—they affect one another. He was delighted with his work, except the equations pointed to the universe having a beginning. Since he believed that could not be true, he inserted a constant, or a fudge factor, to make the universe appear static and eternal.[6]

One of Einstein's great attributes, besides his genius, was his willingness to tell people how to prove or disprove his theory. He stated that if you viewed a known star during a solar eclipse, you could measure how far the Sun's mass bent the observed light. Isaac Newton's laws (the conventional laws of physics) predicted the Sun's gravity would curve the light (photons) coming from the known star a slight amount. General relativity predicted the space-time fabric would bend the light an additional amount. There was just such a solar eclipse in 1919. Scientists measured the amount the light was bent and found it consistent with what Einstein's theory predicted. Einstein was finally hailed as the genius he was, and he was also turning traditional physics on its head. Mathematicians and physicists were already starting to question his cosmological constant, though. They knew that the constant's value was determined to make the universe look static and eternal, but nothing at the time dictated the given value except somebody's preconceived notion.

The game-changer in all this was when Edwin Hubble, in 1929 at the Mount Wilson Observatory, observed a redshift in all known galaxies. Seeing the color red at the edge of every galaxy suggests all the galaxies are moving away because red is the elongated part of the spectrum. The principle is the same as when a train's whistle gets higher and higher pitched as it comes towards you. Compressed sound waves produce a high-frequency noise. Then, when the train goes away from you, the whistle sounds lower-pitched because the sound waves are elongated. The change in frequency due to movement is known as the Doppler effect. If all the galaxies were moving toward us, we would see light from the more compressed, blue side of the spectrum. The redshift confirmed that the universe was indeed moving out and away, so it was not static and eternal.

If you wind the video backward, everything had to have exploded out from a single point. The poor, stupid people who thought the universe had a beginning were actually correct. Albert Einstein finally visited Edwin Hubble's observatory above Los Angeles in 1931. When Einstein saw the redshift himself, he stated that his cosmological constant was the greatest blunder of his life.[7] I mention all this because educated people need to know why we know the universe is expanding. Also, this is an excellent example showing that science does not always interpret the data—scientists do. Scientists, like all people, are human and have built-in, preconceived notions or prejudices. Established dogma is especially difficult to overcome.

A FINELY TUNED UNIVERSE

There are other ways scientists now know the universe had a beginning and is expanding away from us. They theorized early on after Hubble's observations that the universe's origin should have inflated out of a great fireball explosion type event. A natural consequence of the explosion predicted some type of background radiation everywhere in the universe, like a residual afterglow from the blast. In 1965, two scientists, Penzias and Wilson, invented an instrument to measure in those frequencies and discovered that exact afterglow everywhere in the universe and in the wavelength they were estimating. Their research and discovery of the Cosmic Microwave Background (CMB) led to a Nobel Prize in 1978.

Between 1989 and 1993, the COBE satellite (not named after Kobe Bryant, but instead stands for Cosmic Background Explorer) measured the spectrum of the radiation field hundreds of times more accurately than before. The data the satellite beamed back confirmed both Einstein's equations and Penzias and Wilson's. The Hubble telescope, named after the previously mentioned Edwin Hubble of redshift fame, was launched in 1990 and has given us even more accurate readings of the universe. In 1998 scientists finally nailed down the universe's expansion rate and assigned a fairly accurate number to the cosmological constant. They now know it was decelerating the first half of its history and is now accelerating at an increased rate the second half of its history. So, Einstein was correct about a needed constant. He was just incorrect in assigning a constant that made the universe look static and eternal when the rest of his equations had pointed to an expanding universe. In the last 20 years, further experiments have confirmed Einstein's general relativity to a probability of error of one part in 100 trillion. Therefore, it is the most accurately tested theory in all of science.[8]

Einstein, in his genius, already saw the fine-tuning in the universe 100 years ago.[9] In the last 25 years, we have gained a massive amount of scientific evidence that backs up, even more, the fact that the universe is remarkably fine-tuned, or it either would not exist at all or would not support life.[10] For instance, the universe's expansion rate points to something called dark energy that accounts for 69% of our entire universe.[11] Dark energy is the self-stretching property of the space-time fabric, or surface, of the universe. Some scientists equate it with the cosmological constant. It turns out that this dark energy (the expansion rate of the universe) has to be perfect as in 1 in 1×10^{122} perfect, or the whole thing collapses back in on top of itself, or it expands out too quickly and prevents galaxy formation.[12] There are over 100 more of these finely tuned occurrences, and I will mention a few.

The age of the universe is just right to allow stars like our Sun to exist. The speed of light is perfect, or stars would be too luminous or not luminous enough. The average distance between galaxies allows star formation. The decay rate of a proton and the decay rate of Beryllium is precisely right. The ratio of exotic to ordinary matter, Big Bang ripples, and total mass density ensures the universe does not collapse and allows galaxies to form. The temperature in the universe seconds after the

Big Bang was just right to build nuclei from protons and neutrons. The four forces (strong nuclear force, weak nuclear force, electromagnetic force, and gravity) encompass a very narrow range.[13] Particle masses and the spin of the electron and quarks can hardly vary from their existing parameters.[14] There are at least 100 more of these finely tuned occurrences. It is difficult to list them all.

Then, there are also perfect requirements for a planet (Earth, for example), it's moon (i.e., our moon), it's star (i.e., the Sun), and it's galaxy (like the Milky Way) for life of any kind to exist. The galaxy mass, type, and location in the universe have to be at precise limits. The Sun's age, star mass, and solar wind have to be near perfect. There are very narrow limits for the Earth's gravity, distance to the Sun, inclination of orbit, axial tilt, rotation period, magnetic field, thickness of the crust, and the atmosphere's exact makeup. The Earth's oceans, atmosphere, and land surface changed continuously and dramatically through its history. The changes counteracted one another in remarkable ways. A warming trend as small as 1°C every hundred million years would have been enough to make our world uninhabitable by now.[15] There are a multitude more of these type parameters that had to be perfect.

If we go back 30 or 40 years, scientists knew a few parameters had to be perfect for life's existence. In the last 25 years, though, the list has grown substantially to well over 600. The probability of finding a planet that can support microbial life lasting for at least 90 days is 10^{-333}. The probability of a planet supporting intelligent, high-technology physical life is 10^{-1032}. To get some perspective, consider that a one in a trillion trillion trillion trillion trillion trillion trillion trillion chance is written as 10^{-96}. You quickly get a grasp of how unlikely life is anywhere in the universe.[16] Few people anticipated scientists would discover this staggering amount of fine-tuning in our solar system, galaxy, and the universe. It is so finely tuned that it is hard to comprehend and, thus, represents another breathtaking surprise in scientific discovery over the last two decades. I will speak more about the implications of these extraordinary scientific findings in the next chapter.

WHAT IS UP WITH PENCIL LEAD

There is one last scientific discovery we need to discuss because few people are aware of how this breakthrough may significantly influence the 21st century. In 2010 University of Manchester physicists Andre Geim and Konstantin Novoseluv earned the Nobel Prize in physics for discovering a way to produce a material called graphene. As the story goes, they played around in the lab with some adhesive tape and graphite (yes, as in pencil lead). They wondered why they could not create thin carbon layers using tape. They used the "scotch tape" method to extract graphite and put it on an underlying material. The carbon atoms were laid out in a hexagonal pattern as little as one atom thick (thus a two-dimensional material), and graphene was born.

Graphene is up to 200 times stronger than steel, can conduct electricity 25 times faster than silicon at room temperature, and thin sheets are transparent. There are thousands of patents on multiple continents focused on the material. The number of possible applications is staggering. Graphene's potential uses include improving materials, electronics, filters, sensors, battery storage, solar cell efficiency, biotechnology, and a host of others.[17] Scientists and engineers already use the material in small amounts in many of these areas.

Graphene is also incredibly hard to mass-produce. However, researchers continue to make ground in the production phase. A highly respected team of researchers at Rice University recently announced a way to make bulk quantities of lower grade graphene called flash graphene. Low-grade graphene has immediate application in strengthening materials and as a paint additive. According to *Science Magazine*:

> Researchers at Rice University report today in Nature that they <u>can zap virtually any source of solid carbon</u> from food scraps to old car tires, and turn it into graphene—sheets of carbon atoms prized for applications ranging from high-strength plastic to flexible electronics. Current techniques yield tiny quantities of picture-perfect graphene or up to tons of less prized graphene chunks; the new method already produces grams per day of near-pristine graphene in the lab, and researchers are now scaling it up to kilograms per day.[18]

Before long, they will probably also develop ways to manufacture higher-quality graphene in greater quantities. When that happens, there will truly be an explosion in the number of ways it is used.

One of those prime uses is likely to be battery storage and solar cell efficiency. Another possible use is in a membrane that allows hydrogen extraction from the air for use in a hydrogen fuel cell (Andre Geim has already demonstrated this in the lab). I cannot wait for the day the world no longer uses carbon-based fuels. One of my main reasons for bringing to light these new technological breakthroughs is to make people aware that it will not be long before the planet uses renewable energy in increasing amounts. If not in solar power or hydrogen fuel cells, scientists may develop other technologies such as Traveling Wave Reactors advocated by Bill Gates.

The question becomes: do we want to practically stop life as we know it to abandon fossil fuel usage when upcoming technologies can solve the problem for us? Some are saying that we do not have much time, and we have to take drastic action now. Always be wary of people in power whose motto is, "Never waste a crisis." One of the problems is that if there is not a crisis, they will make one as they grab more and more power. The Secretary-General of the World Meteorological Organization, Petteri Taalss, recently stated, "Climate change is not going to be the end of the world... The atmosphere promoted by the media promotes anxiety. The latest idea is that children are a negative thing. I am worried for young mothers, who are already under much pressure. This will only add to their burden."[19] He is obviously very concerned with global warming but goes on to say that he is also worried about extremists on both sides of the issue doing much harm.

We need to be good stewards of the planet and keep it as clean as possible, always striving to do better. This is a pertinent example of the necessity for younger generations to study the science involved, look at both sides of the issues, and make informed decisions. In fact, this entire chapter on science, and recent scientific discoveries, is really about the reader gaining enough knowledge about current events so leaders, who have other agendas other than science, will not lead you astray.

Remember, scientists are mostly good, hard-working people just trying to do their job. Like all people, however, they can have a preconceived bias that affects their conclusions. In the next chapter, we will discuss how some of the previously mentioned scientific discoveries can influence a person's worldview.

7

WORLDVIEWS

Riverboat Gamblers

IF YOU GO BACK TO the mid-1800s, travel in the United States was substantially different. There were few roads in the central part of the country, and those were potholed and dusty. The railroads had not had time to crisscross large parts of the nation. The dramatic westward expansion, fueled by the railroads, did not occur until after the Civil War. Since many of the larger towns often grew up along major rivers, riverboats were a necessary form of travel. These steam-powered boats usually had two decks. Both decks were above the waterline allowing the craft to ride on top of the water and clear sandbars or shallow channels. The main level was where bulk cargo, barrels, and perhaps a few animals were loaded first since their transport paid most of the bills. Once the freight was on board, the main deck passengers hurried on to the deck to find a comfortable spot. Those passengers who might have been a little older, or simply had time to accumulate some assets, paid double the price and took their places on the upper deck. The upper deck passengers actually slept in a small cabin and were able to spend time and eat meals in the large saloon and restaurant.

A person traveling the Mississippi River from New Orleans to St. Louis (or anywhere else up or down a major river) would more than likely find themselves on one of these riverboats. Once out of sight of the city, there was not much to see for long stretches, just endless trees along the shore and occasional passing boats. On a hot, summer day, you can imagine the feel of humidity coming off the river as you take in innocent-looking clouds slowly growing in the distance. The steam engine and paddle wheel's rhythmic sound would mix with the pungent smells of animals and manure, coal smoke, and body odor. When you think of this kind of olfactory assault, you can speculate smoked tobacco of any kind might smell good in comparison; perfume–otherworldly. Chugging along at about 15mph, travelers would try to pass the time any way they could. One of the favorite ways to pass the time for those on the upper deck was to gamble.

Many professional gamblers were run out of various towns by either legislation or their conduct, but the unregulated riverboats were a safe refuge. When you gamble for a living, there is probably no better gift than a captive audience who is somewhat bored. The temptations were considerable, and sometimes the dice were loaded, or there were hidden cards found in dangerous places. There were good reasons some gamblers carried a Deringer up their sleeve. When not gambling with cards or dice, they were betting that yet another boiler explosion, runaway fire, or collision with one too many submerged logs would not destroy the boat. A riverboat only lasted four to five years on the Mississippi and two years on the Missouri River. They gambled in many different ways. The most brazen of risk-takers found their home on these boats. Thus, the expression "like a riverboat gambler" made its way into the English language.

Concerning worldviews and religion, many people resemble those riverboat gamblers. The reason I say they are gambling, and gambling recklessly, is because so many people base their religious beliefs on what they feel should be true, what their friends or family say, or just guesswork. They never have set out to investigate and study which beliefs actually stand up to scrutiny. It makes me think of someone standing at the top of a 40-foot cliff jutting out over a river. They feel like jumping off because of the fun involved, and they would look really awesome. Friends watching the action assure the person that they will definitely secure their place in the cool crowd if they jump. The person looks down and guesses the water is deep enough. Pride is welling up within them as they think about how they get to do it their way. For some strange reason, they do not consider going down and checking out the actual depth of the water. We all need to investigate the depth of our worldview.

Many people are like those riverboat gamblers. Instead of dice and cards, the game is Russian roulette, and instead of only one of the six chambers loaded, five of the six chambers are loaded. Instead of gambling with one's life, they are gambling with eternity. A six-chambered revolver is used as an illustration because there are probably six different religions or worldviews that dominate the landscape. The six could include Christianity, Judaism, Islam, Hinduism, Buddhism, and atheism. They all make mutually exclusive claims, so they cannot all be true. In fact, only one can logically be true, and that is why only one barrel is not loaded. Upon reflection, their bets go well beyond the wagers of a riverboat gambler.

This does not appear wise. The statistics are startling. One hundred percent of all people die, and few people know exactly when. As they say, no one gets out of here alive. The vast majority of people on the planet believe, or sense that there is something after death. A rational person should investigate thoroughly. Perhaps some people think religion is all about blind faith and so there is nothing to check out. This is clearly not true. As long as a religion or a worldview makes a truth claim, then that claim is open to scrutiny using science, logic, and reason.

I will define faith as trusting what you have reason to believe is true. It requires trust, reason, belief, and truth. Faith, then, is not blind unless it is not supported by anything. Faith does cover a gap in knowledge, though. We do not know all things, and because of this gap in knowledge, all worldviews require faith. However, we do have knowledge of many things; and based on that knowledge and reason, we can look at different worldviews and determine which are the most trustworthy. I am certainly not going to tell you what to believe or what to think. I am encouraging you, though, to think. Most people are pretty smart and have a certain amount of innate intelligence that enables them to come to sound conclusions based on the facts and evidence available. With this in view, we will delve into some of the options.

WORLDVIEWS

The term worldview can mean a lot of different things to various people. We will use worldview to refer to a person's perspective on how they view and make sense of the world around them. It reflects how you would answer all the important questions of human existence. The American philosopher and theologian Francis Schaeffer states:

There is a flow to both history and culture. This flow is
rooted and has its wellspring in the thoughts of people.
People are unique in the inner life of the mind – what
they are in their thought world determines how they act.
This is true of their value systems and it is true of their
creativity. It is true of their corporate actions, such as
political decisions, and it is true of their personal lives...
Presuppositions rest upon that which a person considers
to be the truth of what exists. People's presuppositions
lay a grid for all they bring forth into the external world...
The inner thought world determines the outward action.[1]

Your worldview is like a sieve of presuppositions that allows
you to retain particular ideas and eliminate others. Everyone has
a worldview. For our purposes, there are three primary ones:
theism, pantheism, and atheism. All the world religions can fit
under one of these three overall worldviews. Theism is the belief that there is a god or gods. Pantheism believes that god is
in everything in our physical world—god is everything and everything is god, and god is not personal. Atheism is defined as
the belief that there is no god or gods. In the United States, tax
dollars are only allowed to fund schools that teach from an atheist worldview centered curriculum. The number of subgroups of
the three worldviews is almost endless; but if we focus initially
on the truth claims of the three major ones, we can narrow down
some of the further options.

We will start by examining atheism and theism because their
difference is so apparent and easily defined. Is there evidence
for some type of transcendent being or not? Philosophically you
cannot absolutely prove there is a god. Also, philosophically,
you cannot absolutely prove there is no god. However, we can

look at the trend line of accumulated knowledge over the last 25 years and see which direction it points.

I was mostly an atheist until age 27. At the time, I was convinced scientists knew precisely how the universe began, how first life began, and how macroevolution created all the different plants and animals. Since I love science and the scientific method, I was quite surprised by what science unveiled in these three areas over the last couple of decades. Much of the heavy mental work involved in sorting this out was already covered in the previous chapter, but there are a few new items to mention as we progress.

FIRST LIFE

As an atheist, I was sure first life sprang out of some sort of primordial soup billions of years ago. At the time, this did not seem impossible, given enough organic compounds over millions of years. In 1953 the Miller-Urey experiment even demonstrated that random sparks applied to the organic compounds they thought existed 4 billion years ago could produce 5 of the 20 amino acids. They have since found that the early Earth composition was different than what scientists believed in 1953, and amino acids may not form as readily as they thought. But that is not incredibly relevant to first life anyway. As we looked at earlier, a small, modest usable protein, or Pro-machine as I called it, consists of at least 150 amino acids (all left-handed) assembled in perfect order. The mathematical odds of this happening by chance are 1 in 1×10^{74}.[2] This is mathematically impossible. However, the problem is a lot worse since all of life as we know it consists of at least one cell made from a wide variety of complex proteins.

The cells are controlled by a digital base-4 information process-ing system (i.e., DNA) far more elaborate than man has ever produced. Thinking this all came about by random accidental processes is like finding the newest version of an iPhone washed up on the beach. You pick it up and examine it and determine that this sophisticated computer just came together in the ocean via random processes over a long time. This example does not do the problem justice because an iPhone cannot repair itself, regulate all its own processes, or reproduce itself. The simplest life forms can do all these things and are tremendously more complicated. The following quote shows just how bleak the problem is:

> James Tour is a leading origin-of-life researcher with over 630 research publications and over 120 patents. He was inducted into the National Academy of Inventors in 2015, listed in "The World's Most Influential Scientific Minds" by Thomson Reuters in 2014, and named "Scientist of the Year" by R&D Magazine. Here is how he recently de-scribed the state of the field: "We have no idea how the molecules that compose living systems could have been devised such that they would work in concert to fulfill biol-ogy's functions. We have no idea how the basic set of mol-ecules, carbohydrates, nucleic acids, lipids and proteins were made and how they could have coupled in proper se-quences, and then transformed into the ordered assemblies until there was the construction of a complex biological system, and eventually to that first cell. Nobody has any idea on how this was done when using our commonly un-derstood mechanisms of chemical science. Those that say that they understand are generally wholly uninformed re-garding chemical synthesis. Those that say, "Oh this is well

worked out," they know nothing—nothing—about chemical synthesis—nothing.... From a synthetic chemical perspective, neither I nor any of my colleagues can fathom a
prebiotic molecular route to construction of a complex system. We cannot even figure out the prebiotic routes to the
basic building blocks of life: carbohydrates, nucleic acids,
lipids, and proteins. Chemists are collectively bewildered.
Hence I say that no chemist understands prebiotic synthesis
of the requisite building blocks, let alone assembly into a
complex system. That's how clueless we are. I have asked
all of my colleagues—National Academy members, Nobel
Prize winners—I sit with them in offices. Nobody understands this. So if your professors say it's all worked out, if
your teachers say it's all worked out, they don't know what
they're talking about."[3]

He sits in offices with other National Academy members and
Nobel Prize winners, and none of them have a clue where first
life sprang from? So much for understanding where life came
from in regards to an atheistic worldview. Atheist scientists are
still very committed to finding a random, materialistic origin of
life and continue speculating on how it might have happened.
However, in many ways, they almost appear unconcerned about
how first life came about because they just know evolution did
everything once it arrived.

*MACRO*EVOLUTION

*Micro*evolution is a change within species that does not invoke
significant increases in functional genetic information. Some

examples are bacteria developing antibiotic resistance, color, and size differences in a species, or finches developing larger and stronger beaks during a drought because of harder seeds. Microevolution is also known as adaptation and accounts for changes we see at the species and genus levels. No one disputes microevolution, or we would not go to the gym or a tanning salon or selectively breed dogs, horses, or other plants and animals.

However, *macro*evolution involves developing novel body plans and organs through small incremental steps and ultimately requires a massive increase in functional genetic *information*. This is the kind of enormous change we see at the phyla, class, order, and family level. No one has ever observed macroevolution. I know many people believe macroevolution is settled science. For quite a long time, the scientific community has told us that every life form, from hummingbirds to elephants, all evolved from a common single-celled ancestor primarily by the mechanisms of random mutation (and genetic drift) and natural selection. Atheist scientists rigidly and dogmatically believe this because their whole worldview falls apart without it. They try to silence anyone who differs from their opinion.

We must remember that 100 years ago, scientists also did not want to believe the universe had a beginning. Einstein's theory of general relativity, along with Hubble's discovery of the redshift, started the ball rolling; and there was no stopping the collapse of the belief in a static and eternal universe. Many recent breakthroughs in the realm of biochemistry and microbiology have started the ball rolling towards the collapse of the theory of macroevolution. I know this is difficult for some people to comprehend. I, too, was a staunch believer in macroevolution. I realize how hard it is to discover that a firmly held belief has little scientific merit. We will now peruse some of the recent scientific research and writings.

In 1996 Dr. Michael Behe, professor of biochemistry at Lehigh University, published his book *Darwin's Black Box*. The central premise of the book is that all of life at the biochemical level is irreducibly complex. Please do not panic about trying to figure out what the term irreducibly complex means. You have the knowledge from the previous chapter to easily understand the concept. The cell manufactures complex Pro-machines (proteins) on ribosomal assembly lines by laying out numerous amino acids in perfect order. The process is not much different than producing a car engine. The completed engine can turn an axle, and since the wheels are attached to the axle, the wheels move to propel the car. However, the individual piston, spark plug, valves, cylinders, gaskets, and other components have no purpose until final engine assembly. Only the completed car engine has a function. A more basic example is the common mousetrap. The wood base, spring, catch, hammer, and holding bar cannot do anything individually. All the pieces require precise final assembly to catch a mouse successfully. The wood base and hammer alone cannot trap a mouse.[4]

A great example in the field of biology is the rotary motor of the bacterial flagellum. The protein parts actually form a stator, rotor, universal joint, driveshaft, whip-like propeller, and several other distinct parts. The individual parts have no function on their own.[5] Functioning together, they form an incredibly efficient rotary motor that can spin at a speed of 100s of turns per second. This is faster than the turbine sections of modern jet engines. The flagellum's whip-like propeller can also reverse directions in an instant. These capabilities are beyond human technological progress and are why biomimetic engineering is becoming very popular. Biomimetics applies our knowledge of engineering, chemistry, and biology to *mimic* biological micro-machines to make human-produced machines more efficient.

Charles Darwin stated that if anyone could show that evolution could not proceed by small incremental steps, then his theory is false. All of life consists of irreducibly complex biochemical machines. DNA itself is irreducibly complex. You need all the parts of the process to make a protein. The entire DNA structure and associated mechanisms require proteins to function. It is mathematically impossible for these systems to assemble by random small steps; therefore, neo-Darwinism is impossible. British philosopher Anthony Flew, a famous atheist advocate and debater of the 20th century, read *Darwin's Black Box* and other research at the time and became a deist in 2004.[6] He said that he simply had to follow the evidence where it led. There was much more evidence to come. In reporting the evidence over the next several pages, some technical terminology is needed, and the technical world we live in demands full coverage. However, the average reader should feel free to scan the information at a level proportional to their professional need or interest.

In 2007 Michael Behe published *The Edge of Evolution*. The book details how we now know the rate at which random mutation can alter DNA and how many protein changes are possible in a given time. Remember, macroevolution says that all species descended from a common ancestor (common descent) via random mutation (and possibly some random genetic drift in small populations) and natural selection. Random mutation in the DNA primarily occurs through environmental hazards like ultraviolet light or certain chemicals or errant copying of DNA during cellular processes. Random mutation in the genome is the prime mover and has to create an inherited change before there is anything to select through natural selection (survival of the fittest).

Therefore, if we know the rate that random mutation occurs, we can determine if there is enough time for a random process to build complex micro-machines, digital base-4 information processing systems, organs, and novel body shapes. I will give you three guesses as to what Dr. Behe discovered. The random mutation rate in the genome is hopelessly too slow to build complex micro-machines, let alone the complex factories that build them. Michael Behe, as a biochemist, studied single-celled organisms like malaria and E. coli. He also studied research data on HIV. These organisms reproduce at the biological speed of light compared to mammals. The numbers of malarial cells produced in a single year are likely 100 times greater than the number of all the mammals that have ever lived on earth in the past 200 million years.[7] By studying these microorganisms, he discovered the rates of random mutation and copying errors could only produce two novel protein to protein binding site changes in the earth's history. Single-celled simple life forms require a minimum of dozens, if not hundreds, of protein to protein binding sites to make them functional.[8] His data and conclusions should not surprise us. No matter how much time there is in the universe, random events cannot possibly build automated biochemical machines and factories.

In 2009, Stephen Meyer (PhD Cambridge University) published his book *Signature in the Cell*. In the book, Meyer details how DNA is digital base-4 functional information that builds things. He also explains how encoded information is useless without a system that can read, translate, and process it. He builds on mathematician William Dembski's previous work showing that complex and specified information does not just appear by random processes.

This whole concept that all of life is constructed, regulated, and propagated by functional *information* is earth-shattering and has far-reaching implications. There is something different about information. A blank magnetic tape weighs just as much as one loaded with new software. Information does not have mass, charge, or length in millimeters. So, matter and information are two separate domains. DNA is the medium; it is not the message.[9] It is amazing to think that information technology and coding theory have been in place in biology for 3.85 billion years.[10] An intelligent mind is the only proven source of complex and specified information.[11]

The accumulating evidence against macroevolution may have prompted highly decorated NYU atheist professor of philosophy Thomas Nagel, in 2012, to publish his book *Mind and Cosmos: Why the Materialist Neo-Darwinian Conception of Nature Is Most Certainly False*. The title says it all and is quite surprising coming from an atheist. In the introduction, he states, "The more details we learn about the chemical basis of life and the intricacy of the genetic code, the more unbelievable the standard historical account becomes."[12] The book goes on to say that philosophers, past or present, have never been able to account for consciousness, cognizance (reason), or value and beauty (morality and art) by purely materialistic causes. On the last page of the book he says:

I have argued patiently against the prevailing form of naturalism, a reductive materialism that purports to capture life and mind through its neo-Darwinian extension. But to go back to my introductory remarks, I find this view antecedently unbelievable – a heroic triumph of ideological theory over common sense. The empirical evidence can be interpreted to accommodate different comprehensive theories, but in this case the cost in conceptual and probabilistic contortions is prohibitive. I would be willing to bet that the present right-thinking consensus will come to seem laughable in a generation or two–though of course it may be replaced by a new consensus that is just as invalid.[13]

Notably, he bets neo-Darwinism will be a laughable theory in a generation or two. Professor Nagel was educated at Cornell and Oxford and received his doctorate from Harvard. I only mention his academic credentials so that people know he is no hack. Someone may complain that both Anthony Flew and Thomas Nagel are both just philosophers, not scientists. However, the basis for the methods of science such as causality, universality, induction, deduction, and abduction are not proven scientifically. They are assumed philosophically. Scientists may not like it, but science is actually a slave to philosophy.

In 2013 Stephen Meyer published another book titled *Darwin's Doubt*, a *New York Times* bestseller. It turns out one of Charles Darwin's main doubts regarding macroevolution was the fact that there were no transitional fossils. Darwin glossed over his doubts, assuming transitional fossils would be found sometime in the future. Paleontologists have searched vigorously for over 160 years since the publication of Darwin's *Origin of Species*. There are still no significant transitional fossils. As paleontologist Stephen Jay Gould of Harvard said, "The extreme rarity of transitional forms in the fossil record persist as the trade secret of paleontology."[14]

This is especially apparent in the Cambrian explosion 540 million years ago, where at least 21 of the 36 phyla appear in a geological instant. Cambria is the Latin name for Wales and is where the fascinating Cambrian fossils were discovered as early as the 1600s. Adam Sedgwick studied under Charles Darwin. In 1831, Sedgwick was the first to detail the significance of the fossils and named them after Cambria.[15]

Two more discoveries confirmed the validity of the Cambrian explosion—the Burgess Shale fossils in British Columbia in 1911 and the Chengjiang fossil site in China in the 1980s. The Chinese discovery demonstrated that sedimentary rocks could preserve soft bodies in exquisite detail.

There was no disputing there was an explosion of advanced body plans that arrived in a very sudden period of only about six million years. At least 21 of the 36 phyla appeared in the equivalent of 1 minute on a 24-hour clock of life's history on earth.[16] We know this is not enough time and a mathematical impossibility since we know the rate of random mutation. Even with significantly more time, do we really think that random processes can introduce enormous quantities of digital base-4 code into an organism's DNA to build organs and body plans? Geneticist John F. McDonald showed that early embryonic mutational changes have never been tolerated in any species, and those are the ones needed for morphological (body plan) change.[17]

But what about all those pictures in the biology textbooks showing man proceeding from monkeys to apes to something in between and then Neanderthal and finally modern man? The star of the show for evolutionists was Piltdown Man. He was discovered in 1912 in Piltdown, England. His traits placed him right in the middle between apes and man. Paleoanthropologists quickly placed the fossil in a secure vault at the Museum of Natural History in London. The museum denied access to those wanting to closely examine the skull. Finally, 41 years later, the museum allowed access and scientists quickly discovered a fraud. Someone had taken a very old human skull and combined it with a filed down and chemically treated jawbone of an orangutan. Piltdown Man is now known as the greatest scientific fraud in the history of the world and, yet, few people know about it. Also, as it turns out, Neanderthal man is the same as modern man. There is not anything now in the intermediate lineup. All the evidence for human evolution between about 5 and 10 million years ago can be fitted into a small box. All the drawings were like bedtime stories for adults.[18]

There are several other pictures in the biology textbooks detailing evolution. The drawings of the similar embryos were actually altered drawings by evolutionist Ernst Hackel. They are now considered fraudulent.[19] The Kettlewell moth experiment was also doctored. Even if it had been legitimate, it would have only demonstrated color change, which we can easily do through selective breeding.[20] Darwin's finches on the Galapagos Island only demonstrated that a drought causes larger birds and bigger beaks to crack hard seeds. They now appear to revert back to their previous condition during normal climates.[21] The tree of life, another popular picture, is in total disarray for many reasons. The main one is the fact that the Cambrian explosion requires massive numbers of intermediates. There are none. The pictures in the biology textbooks were wishful thinking.

In 2016 Douglas Axe (PhD, Chemical Engineering, California Institute of Technology) published his book *Undeniable: How Biology Confirms Our Intuition That Life Is Designed*. He and Ann Gauger (BS in biology from MIT, PhD University of Washington, post-doctoral fellow Harvard) worked with two similar, but different enzymes and tested millions of random mutations. They could not get enzyme A (Kbl) to evolve its function into enzyme B (BioF).[22] I cited his book earlier concerning the fact that he found there is only one good protein sequence for every 10^{74} bad ones. Proteins are very finicky, and unless their amino acid parts are all left-handed and laid out almost perfectly, they will not fold to make a functional protein. Macro evolutionists try to ascribe intelligent properties to natural selection, but natural selection can only select something that is already modified. Therefore, random mutation or other random processes have to perform all the creative work.[23]

To make matters worse for neo-Darwinists, in early 2019, Michael Behe showed that mutations are almost always destructive and thus extremely limited in what they can accomplish. In what has to be a classic quote, he states:

> Rather than guiding the construction of elegant biological machinery, selection predominately scavenges a junkyard of broken or degraded parts. Degrading machinery can be useful for some purposes – perhaps because its function is unneeded at the time, and so the scrapped machine doesn't waste energy; or because in changed circumstances the product the machine made is now detrimental; or some other reason. But natural selection can't build a coherent new system any more than a pack rat can.[24]

Only in the last 20 years has science advanced enough to examine life in the molecular detail necessary to test Darwin's ideas rigorously. Since even the smallest need for coordination is a huge problem for random evolution, complex structures are beyond the reach of Darwinian processes.[25] Neo-Darwinists/ macro evolutionists desperately propose theories like the multiverse and self-organization. The multiverse is not science. And biochemists can assure you organic compounds do not self-organize to form life.

THE DEFECTION

As evidence against macroevolution accumulates, more and more scientists are defecting. There are now more than a thousand PhD scientists who have signed a statement titled "A Scientific Dissent from Darwinism." The pronouncement states, "We are skeptical of claims for the ability of random mutation and natural selection to account for the complexity of life. Careful examination of the evidence for Darwinian theory should be encouraged."[26] You can go online and check it out. When you do, make sure you also go to Wikipedia and see what they have to say about it. Someone stated once that young college students and grad assistants maintain most Wikipedia entries. They sit by the computer continuously to make sure no one tries to change their favorite professor's biased position on some topic. It is for good reason Wikipedia is not allowed as an authority or reference in serious writings.

Wikipedia is, as a whole, profoundly one-sided in favor of macroevolution and stomachs no evidence to the contrary. With that in view, it is almost comical to read what they say about "A Scientific Dissent from Darwinism." The words *frantic* and *extreme fear* comes to mind. With great fear, they frantically quote lobbying groups like NCSC or resort to name-calling or incorrect categorization. A favorite tactic is categorizing anyone who opposes macroevolution as a creationist or trying to give them some other label. When you see this level of fear and desperation, you can be assured they come from people defending a theory in trouble. When someone is confident about their position, they engage with facts and sound arguments—not name-calling.

The numerous defenders of Darwinism remind me of the proverbial agitated traffic cops overseeing a train wreck. People have stopped and are getting out of their cars to take a look. The cops tell everyone to move along; there's nothing to see here. If you dawdle a little, they start yelling at you and calling you names (I have never seen real traffic cops call anyone names, but the Internet traffic cops certainly will). They are yelling at you and calling you names because there really is something to see here as a theory starts to go up in flames.

Apparently, David Gelernter, an accomplished professor of computer science at Yale University, had seen enough. In the spring of 2019, he published his essay, "Giving up Darwin: a fond farewell to a brilliant and beautiful theory."[27] It is a great little essay and well worth reading. Add another name to the dissent list. Of course, now if you reference Dr. Gelernter on the internet, you will already see the subtle name-calling or categorizations as an extremist of some sort. These are the tactics of people who are very insecure and threatened.

The normal question to ask is why they feel so threatened if they are presently the majority position. There are probably many reasons. We know it is relatively common for people to get agitated when their worldview is threatened. Also, people in power do not like having their power and prestige jeopardized. Publishing peer-reviewed literature is a huge deal in the academic community. Scientists and professors who hold tightly to macroevolution have held tremendous power in determining who gets to be peer-reviewed and who does not. Lastly, never forget how people react when something imperils their research funding. Did someone say money? As much as we would like to have a rational debate based on facts and evidence, these are the reasons we can expect to get an emotional response instead.

I have thoroughly read the previous books and many others. The authors make extremely sound arguments based on scientific evidence, logic, and reason, and one should take them very seriously. Their conclusions have not been refuted. As I stated earlier, their opponents try to label them as creationists. In reality, almost all the scientists referenced are not trying to make a theological statement. They are simply stating that all the evidence points to design by a conscious mind. We can test for the presence of complex and specified functional information, and when we find it, we know from observation that it is always the result of an intelligent agent. However, they leave it up to the individual to decide if the conscious mind is from an alien or a transcendent being or something else. They do readily acknowledge, though, that their research and conclusions have significant worldview implications.

THE IMPLICATIONS OF DESIGN IN LIVING THINGS

As we step back and look at the accumulating evidence over the last 25 years, the trend vector points enormously towards design in life. I never anticipated this amount of evidence coming out in such a short time. The complexity and informational storage capacity of DNA is astounding. In 2015 scientists estimated they could store all the information in the world in a teaspoon of DNA. There is a race on now to utilize DNA for information storage since it far exceeds our current data storage capabilities. The three billion base pairs of DNA in a single human cell (when laid out, not even stretching it) measures a little over six feet. Six feet multiplied by the nearly 40 trillion cells of one person means the DNA of a single human would extend to the sun and back 200 times. Also, it is integrated perfectly into a myriad of systems and subsystems, or we would not live. The human brain has about 86 billion neurons and somewhere between 100 trillion and 1,000 trillion synapses (connections). In 2010, Dr. Stephen Smith led a Stanford research project exploring the brain. He states, "A single human brain has more switches than all the computers and routers and Internet connections on earth."[28]

A person might respond, "So what, it sounds like you're just saying it is all very complex." Yes, but it is also a complexity made possible by encoded information. The cell is utilizing a digital information processing system that reflects our most advanced computer science on steroids. It all points to an intelligent mind. One still has to determine if it was an alien or a transcendent being. Francis Crick, a co-discoverer of the DNA molecule, avoided theistic implications by hypothesizing that life was somehow deposited here on an asteroid. However, you still have to ask where that life originated. In the next section, we will further narrow down theistic versus atheistic possibilities.

CREATION OF THE UNIVERSE

People tend to believe, as I did, that scientists know exactly how the universe began. We should give astrophysicists great credit; they have unraveled quite a bit. From the previous chapter, we know that scientists have confirmed the universe had a definite beginning. *Encyclopedia Britannica* is not an entirely bad source to cite regarding generally accepted views concerning its inception. At least they have real editors. They state:

> According to the big-bang model, the universe expanded rapidly from a highly compressed primordial state, which resulted in a significant decrease in density and temperature. Soon afterward, the dominance of matter over anti-matter (as observed today) may have been established by processes that also predict proton decay. During this stage many types of elementary particles may have been present. After a few seconds, the universe cooled enough to allow the formation of certain nuclei. The theory predicts that definite amounts of hydrogen, helium, and lithium were produced. Their abundances agree with what is observed today. About one million years later the universe was sufficiently cool for atoms to form. The radiation that also filled the universe was then free to travel through space. This remnant of the early universe is the cosmic microwave background radiation—the "three degree" (actually 2.728 K) background radiation—discovered in 1965 by American physicists Arno A. Penzias and Robert W. Wilson.[29]

Astronomer Fred Hoyle came up with the term Big Bang in 1950 to describe the theory of a sudden beginning to the universe. He was not a fan of the theory because of its theistic implications and had proposed a steady-state infinite universe instead. Big Bang conjures up visions of an extremely random event, but now we know the initial expansion of the universe was perfect. For every billion antiparticles in the early universe, there were a billion *and one* particles. The "billion" antiparticles canceled out 1 billion particles to leave *one* extra particle out of every billion. Billions of these leftover particles formed the matter in our universe. The incredible precision allowed star formation and the production of the right number of protons and neutrons to ensure an adequate quantity of the elements essential for life.[30] From Chapter 6, we know everything expanded out in a manner so that over 600 parameters are exact enough to allow life to exist. The odds of this happening to enable a planet to support microbial life is 10^{-333}, and the odds of it allowing a planet supporting advanced life is 10^{-1032}.[31]

In hindsight, perhaps the beginning of the universe should have been called the Great Infinitely Fine Tuned appearance, like trillions of symphonies playing in perfect harmony simultaneously the music of time, space, and matter as it all surges out to make a universe from nothing. By 1992 Fred Hoyle had changed his perspective. When asked if he thought a supernatural intelligence was guiding the universe, he nodded in agreement. "That's the way I look on God. It's a fix, but how it's being fixed I don't know."[32]

Scientists still do not know. There is just no way to know what happened before 10^{-43} seconds.[33] We do know, however, that there was a beginning and, thus, a cause for that beginning. The extreme fine-tuning points to a transcendent being beyond time, space, and matter that is infinitely more powerful than anything we can imagine. The atheist is forced to believe that nothing created all this order out of nothing. Their position is now so dire they have to revert to the hypothesis of a multiverse. The multiverse is the belief in an infinite number of universes, and we just happen to live in the one where everything is perfect for life. This theory is pure metaphysics since there is no evidence of another universe whatsoever. Even if there were, I can't imagine the amount of fine-tuning required for the imagined infinite universe generator. It appears the rational person must consider some form of theism because an all-powerful being decided to create all of this order out of nothing. The omnipotent being, then, also decided to create life as well since the probability of first life coming from random causes is outside the realm of mathematical possibility. Macroevolution cannot account for massive increases in genetic information able to generate novel organs and body plans.

Pantheism falls apart because the transcendent being has to be outside of time, space, and matter (not part of it) to create this universe out of nothing. There is no pantheistic worldview that has rationally accounted for the beginning of the universe. Polytheistic religions also do not rationally account for the first cause.[34] Also, the transcendent being appears to be omnipotent (all-powerful), and many "omnipotent" gods are contradictory.[35] We have narrowed it down to monotheism, so which monotheistic religion do we now choose?

CHRISTIANITY, JUDAISM OR ISLAM

The two largest religions in the world just happen also to be monotheistic. Christianity is the largest, with about 2.3 billion followers making up roughly 30% of the world's population. Christians regard both the Old Testament and the New Testament of the *Bible* as the inspired word of God. Islam is the second-largest with about 1.8 billion adherents, which is close to 24% of the world's population. Islam considers the *Quran* as revealed to Mohammed in the seventh century as their holiest book. Judaism only has about 14 million followers making up only .2% of the world's population. Judaism bases their religion only on the Old Testament of the Bible, which they call the Tanakh. All three religions regard Abraham as their patriarch and are appropriately named the Abrahamic faiths.

So far, we have approached the question of worldview using science, logic, and reason. Continuing along those lines, one might ask if a rational God would distinguish the one true monotheistic religion from all the others. If so, how might he do so? One possible way is to describe the initial creation of the universe in surprising detail and accuracy far beyond human knowledge available at the time of the writing. This is what we see in Genesis 1 of the Old Testament believed by Christians and Jews. Some scientists have observed that the six-day Genesis description compares remarkably well to what scientists are finding true about the initial beginnings of our universe and solar system.[36] The Hebrew word for day used in Genesis 1 is *yom* and can mean an extended length of time.[37] No other religions spell it out like this. In fact, most of them are silent or esoteric and vague.

There is another distinctive way that it appears God has put his signature exclusively on Christianity's truth claims and that is the presence of fulfilled prophecy. Over 100 prophecies concerning the Messiah in the Old Testament were written somewhere between 1500 BC and 430 BC. The odds of one person accidentally fulfilling just eight of the hard prophecies is 1 in 10^{17}. Someone described those odds as the same as covering Texas in silver dollars 2 feet deep and then traveling around for days and reaching out and picking up one specially marked silver dollar.[38] So the odds of accidentally fulfilling just eight prophecies are incredibly remote—yet alone 20 or 30 prophecies predicting the where, what, when, and how of some future event. If these prophecies are correct, then Christianity is the rational choice.

DEAD SEA SCROLLS

How do we know the Old Testament was not written or changed hundreds of years after Christ to make it look like he fulfilled these prophecies? Well, the Dead Sea Scrolls (also called the Qumran Scrolls) were found in 1946 by Bedouin shepherds. These scrolls contained parts, or sometimes all, of the 39 books in the Old Testament except Esther. The oldest, most numerous, and most complete book found was the book of Isaiah. Scholars dated the oldest of the 21 copies of Isaiah to 150 BC based on both carbon dating and manuscript dating using things like known punctuation, types of abbreviations, and special letters. No one disputes the dating of the Dead Sea Scrolls. The scrolls are word for word compared with the Old Testament we have today, except for some variations in spellings and a few slips of the pen. The find at Qumran dismisses Islam's claim, or anyone else's, that the Old Testament was changed.

Finding the complete book of Isaiah is highly significant because Isaiah Chapter 53 has more messianic prophecies in one place than any other Old Testament Scripture. Some people are a bit surprised when they read it for the first time. The relevant passages actually start in Isaiah 52:13 and go through 53:12.

Isaiah 52:13-15
13. See, my servant will act wisely; he will be raised and lifted up and highly exalted.
14. Just as there were many who were appalled at him—his

appearance was so disfigured beyond that of any man and his form marred beyond human likeness—so will he sprinkle many nations, and kings will shut their mouths because of him.

15. For what they were not told, they will see, and what they had not heard, they will understand.

Isaiah 53:1-12

1. Who has believed our message and to whom has the arm of the Lord been revealed?

2. He grew up before him like a tender shoot, and like a root out of dry ground. He had no beauty or majesty to attract us to him, nothing in his appearance that we should desire him.

3. He was despised and rejected by mankind, a man of suffering, and familiar with pain. Like one from whom people hide their faces he was despised, and we held him in low esteem.

4. Surely he took up our pain and bore our suffering, yet we considered him punished by God, stricken by him, and afflicted.

5. But he was pierced for our transgressions, he was crushed for our iniquities; the punishment that brought us peace was on him, and by his wounds we are healed.

6. We all, like sheep, have gone astray, each of us has turned to our own way; and the Lord has laid on him the iniquity of us all.

7. He was oppressed and afflicted, yet he did not open his mouth; he was led like a lamb to the slaughter, and as a sheep before its shearers is silent, so he did not open his mouth.

8. By oppression and judgment he was taken away. Yet who of his generation protested? For he was cut off from the land of the living; for the transgression of my people he was punished.

9. He was assigned a grave with the wicked, and with the rich in his death, though he had done no violence, nor was any deceit in his mouth.

10. Yet it was the Lord's will to crush him and cause him to suffer, and though the Lord makes his life an offering for sin, he will see his offspring and prolong his days, and the will of the Lord will prosper in his hand.

11. After he has suffered, he will see the light of life and be satisfied; by his knowledge my righteous servant will justify many, and he will bear their iniquities.

12. Therefore I will give him a portion among the great, and he will divide the spoils with the strong, because he poured out his life unto death, and was numbered with the transgressors. For he bore the sin of many, and made intercession for the transgressors. (NIV)

There are at least eight prophecies fulfilled by Jesus in just these verses. Many scholars and others do not like the ramifications of Isaiah 53, so they try to say the suffering servant is Israel. Israel is not the suffering servant because the reference is singular, not plural. Also, Israel was not sinless, did not willingly subject itself to anyone, and did not take on the sins of others. The passage is so remarkable that Rabbis traditionally no longer read it in their synagogues. This fact alone probably proves more than anything else that it is truly a messianic prophecy. Christians have great respect for the Jewish people since Jesus and his disciples were all Jewish, and the Jewish people were chosen for the Messiah to be born into. We do wish, however, they would not be reluctant to read Isaiah 53 in their synagogues.

Isaiah 53 is the key to seeing all the Old Testament prophecies because some scholars like to say that many of the other prophecies were simply not referring to the Messiah. However, there is absolutely no doubt that Isaiah 53 does refer to the Messiah. Jesus fulfills every one of those prophecies. Therefore, we can look to the New Testament as truth and then back again to all the other Old Testament prophecies to see that he fulfilled those as well, which unlocks the full unity of the Bible. The fulfilled prophecies, then, separates Christianity from both Judaism and Islam.

FURTHER SORTING

The New Testament also has over 5,600 manuscripts that date very close (by historical standards) to the period. The New Testament documents have more manuscripts, earlier manuscripts, and more abundantly supported manuscripts then the best 10 pieces of classical literature combined.[39] No other religion on the planet has anything like this to back it up. In choosing between Christianity and Islam, I could have mentioned that Jesus taught to love your enemies and Mohammed modeled warfare to spread Islam. Ultimately, you have to judge every religion by its founder. Jesus modeled a life of serving, sacrifice, and loving others. One can easily research Mohammed's ethics and his views towards women and come to your own conclusions. However, in doing so, Christianity teaches that we always treat others with gentleness and respect.

I have covered a great deal of material in our rational analysis of worldviews and religion. In doing so, I am following in the footsteps of 20th-century philosopher Mortimer Adler who wrote the Syntopicon to the *Great Books of the Western World*. He was asked why his section on religion was the largest since he was not known as an especially religious person at the time. He replied that religion affects the five great questions more than any other subject. The five great questions are origin, identity, meaning, morality, and destiny.[40] The middle one, meaning, immediately captures people's attention. People want that one desperately. They seem not to realize that all five are very inter-related, and all five demonstrate the incredible importance of worldview for this life (and the next life for those who believe in eternity). A person's worldview should be accumulative in truthfully answering the five questions. No worldview answers all of them perfectly, but there should be an accumulation of truth over time. A person who knows what they believe and why they believe it has conviction. A great generation will have the conviction to overcome false and destructive ideas.

I have approached this chapter with the view that we should not blindly gamble with anything as important as our worldview and religious beliefs. They truly do impact the great questions of life more than any other category of study. I have laid out a rational path as to why a person could easily choose Christianity as the best possible worldview. I do not at all expect every person to choose a Christian worldview at this point. In fact, many people do not even understand what that entails. We now turn our attention to discovering what true Christianity is.

8

CHRISTIANITY

*Perhaps the Christianity You Have Been
Rejecting Should be Rejected*

KA-CHUNGG. NO MATTER HOW MANY times I go through the successive doors of a prison, I never really get used to that sound. You hear the sound as the first door closes behind you. Then you hear it again after going down a short corridor and the second door closes, the third door closes, a long corridor and the fourth door shuts, and finally the fifth as you go deeper into the prison. There is a sound of echoing finality to it that we usually do not encounter in the natural world around us. Even though I do not like that sound, I really do like volunteering to help those in correctional facilities. Over the years, a couple of things strike me concerning the facility in which I volunteer. The first is the professionalism of the staff. They have a pleasant demeanor, but they are always incredibly professional for obvious reasons. The second thing that stands out is the dedication of the other volunteers I work alongside in the facility. My travel schedule forces me to miss one or two weeks a month. The others just never seem to miss a week, unless perhaps they are sick. Most of them are there every time.

The last door opens into one of the 12 sections. Each section consists of a relatively spacious open area and two floors of cells against the back wall divided by a steel staircase. Each cell door has a colored light by the lock. Green indicates the occupant is allowed to come out of the cell and mingle in the open area. Red means the occupant is not allowed to come out for some reason. I usually have no idea why the inmates are in there, and it is probably better that way. I typically spend time with anywhere from 3-12 men seated at bolted down tables in the section open area.

THE SPECIAL REQUIREMENT

On several occasions, I have had these men ask me what Christianity actually is; or within the context of other conversations, I could tell they had no idea what it is. Over time, I came up with a couple of questions or scenarios to correct some misconceptions about Christian belief. It is early in the morning when we meet. To wake them up and get them to think a little, I will say something provocative like, "There is a special requirement before you can become a Christian. Not just anyone can become a Christian." They almost always look at me quizzically, a little unsure of themselves. You can see them thinking, wondering to themselves. The statement does not sound right. At the same time, they are more than likely thinking, "You probably have to be a fairly good person to be a Christian, and I have done some stuff that might keep me out. I probably needed to go to church every Sunday to qualify," or something along those lines.

I don't keep them in suspense too long and finally tell them to ask me what the special requirement is. They quickly ask,

"What's the special requirement?" I answer, "The special requirement is that you have to be a sinner. Perfect people need not
apply." Immediately false pretenses and misconceptions disap-
pear, and even their countenances seem to change as they realize
we are all in this together. I go on to say that, specifically, you
have to know you are a sinner. The apostle Paul in Romans 3:23
states, "For all have sinned and fall short of the glory of God."
We all qualify, but we have to know that we do qualify. There are
only two types of people in the world concerning sin. Those who
know they are sinners and those who don't know. But we all
are. As G.K. Chesterton noted, "Certain new theologians dispute
original sin, which is the only part of Christian theology which
can really be proved." There are no perfect people out there. It
turns out Jesus was a friend of sinners; in fact, that is one of his
official titles. The self-righteous religious leaders of Jesus' time
wanted nothing to do with him. They hoped to kill him and,
eventually, did. However, tax-gatherers, prostitutes, and others
flocked to him. They had the advantage of knowing deep down
that sinners need to repent, and they also need a Savior–perfect
people do not need either.

This concept of coming to the knowledge of our true condition is best told in the New Testament parable of the prodigal
son in Luke 15:11 – 32. I will paraphrase it slightly. In the story,
a father has two sons. One day the younger son says to his father, "Father, give me my share of the estate." In first-century
Palestine, this would be about the same as saying, "Dad, I wish
you were dead. But since you're not, I want my share of the inheritance now because I'm over it putting up with the way you
do things."

A few days later, the younger son gets all his money and
things together and leaves for a distant land. He immediately

makes lots of friends with his newfound wealth in the neighboring country and spends it lavishly on wild parties. Before long, the money's gone and so are his friends. Then the famine hits. The only job he can find is feeding pigs, and he is so hungry he is dreaming about eating pig food. When he is at the lowest of lows, he finally has what we call an *aha* moment. It dawns on him that his father's hired workers live much better than he does in his current situation. He decides to go back to his father and tell him, "Father, I have sinned against heaven and you. I'm not worthy of being called your son; please make me like one of your hired men." So, he heads out to return home.

His father sees him while he is still a long way off, is filled with compassion, runs to him, hugs him, and kisses him. The son says to his father, "I have sinned against heaven and against you. I'm no longer worthy of being called your son." The father, though, says to his hired workers, "Quick! Bring the best clothes we have and put them on him. Get all the filet mignon and best food out; we are going to have a feast and celebrate. For this son of mine was dead and is alive again; he was lost and is found." So the party begins.

Meanwhile, the older son is out working in the field. When he comes near the house, he hears music and dancing. He calls one of the workers and asks him what is going on. He is told his younger brother has returned, and his father is preparing all the best food because he has him back safe and sound.

The older brother becomes angry and refuses to go in, so his father goes out and pleads with him to join the party. But he answers his father, "Look! All these years I've been slaving for you and never disobeyed your orders. Yet you never even cooked the ribeyes so I could celebrate with my friends. But when this son of yours who has squandered your property with prostitutes comes home, you bring out the best of everything for him!" The father states, "My son, you are always with me, and everything I have is yours. But we had to celebrate and be glad because this brother of yours was dead and is alive again; he was lost and is found."

So it is with all of us when we finally come to the knowledge of our true condition before a holy and perfect God and repent. He lovingly accepts us back, not as servants or slaves, but as sons and daughters of the living God. The most sobering part of the story is that we don't know if the older son, who thought he was perfect, ever went into the party.

The story highlights the first misconception of the Christian faith. Christianity is not for perfect people because none of us are. We all have imperfections and issues. We could never live in a flawless enough manner to earn our way into a relationship with a holy and perfect God. When we come to the knowledge of our true condition and repent, he welcomes us back with open arms. As Christians, we are not proud of our sin, and we want to lead a morally upright life. However, we will never be perfect on this earth. There is the initial repentance, but we will also always have other occasions to repent, pick ourselves up, and do better again.

THE 80% – 20% RULE

The second scenario highlights another insidious misconception of the Christian faith. In this situation, I tell the inmates to imagine that a category four tornado (or a fire with very intense smoke) hits the facility without warning, and we are all dead. Then I ask, "How many of you are 100% sure you are going to heaven?" Sometimes a hand will go up. Then I ask how many are 80%, 50%, 20%, or 0% sure. I usually get hands going up here all over the spectrum. Then I explain to them that our feelings can influence our answer to this question, but the Bible says there are only two possible answers. You are either 100% going to heaven or are at a 0% chance of going to heaven. There is no in-between.

Several of the men next want to know how they can get to 100% assurance, and therefore, we cover some verses out of the New Testament book of Romans that summarize several points of the Christian doctrine. Romans 2:5 says, "But because of your stubbornness and unrepentant heart you are storing up wrath for yourself in the day of wrath and revelation of the righteous judgment of God," If the problem is stubbornness and having an unrepentant heart, what should we do instead? People can figure out pretty quickly after the story of the prodigal son and going over our sinful nature that we need to stop being stubborn and repent.

Romans 6: 23 states, "For the wages of sin is death, but the free gift of God is eternal life in Christ Jesus our Lord." The death referred to here is a spiritual death that separates us from a loving God. Romans 5:8 says, "But God demonstrated his own love for us, in that while we were yet sinners, Christ died for us." God was not surprised by sin entering the world and had a plan for it. The entire Old Testament shows God preparing the way for his only begotten Son to be born into the world to atone for our sins. Then Romans 10: 9,10 states, "that if you confess with your mouth Jesus as Lord, and believe in your heart that God raised Him from the dead, you will be saved; for with the heart a person believes, resulting in righteousness, and with the mouth he confesses, resulting in salvation."

That verse does *not* say, "...**if** you do everything just right the rest of your life." God is not afraid to use the word *if* in the Bible. Someone counted in their Bible and found the word *if* used almost 600 times. You just don't see it, though, after any salvation verses. You don't see it after a salvation verse because Ephesians 2:8, 9 clearly says, "For by grace you have been saved through faith; and that not of yourselves, it is the gift of God; not as a result of works, so that no one may boast." Grace means receiving something much better than we deserve—we cannot earn it on our merit.

God did all the heavy work here. Christians believe in the Trinity. The one God exists in the three forms of the Father, Son, and Holy Spirit. You could think of it possibly as a triangle with three corners. Even though the triangle is one entity, it has three distinct corners. The Father sent the Son to live the perfect life on earth to be the perfect sacrifice for our sins. All we have to do is to repent and believe.

Grace, then, is the one thing that separates Christianity from the other religions on the planet. You cannot work your way to heaven. Most of the other religions are similar to a person thinking that if they do particular things just right, they might work their way to the top of the mountain and someday be with God. Christianity says that God came down from the top of the mountain in the form of the Son to live with us.[1] He came to demonstrate the perfect life, and ultimately bear our sins on the cross. Grace says there is no 80%, 50%, or 20%. We receive what God did for us with open arms, not clinging to any of our good works. By faith we receive, and because God did it, we have 100% assurance. This is guaranteed, and no one can take it from you. This is also unbelievably good news. The Bible says that when you believe in the Son, you are sealed in the Holy Spirit. Who can break God's seal–no one! Once someone understands this concept of unmerited grace and that we cannot work our way to heaven, it clears up the second major misconception of the Christian faith.

Inmates often want to pray to accept Christ but do not know what to say exactly, so I guide them along. I make sure they understand this is something they do because they want to and truly believe it. Those who desire pray something to the effect, "Father God, I have sinned against you in thought, word, and action. I feel sorrow and brokenness for what this sin cost you. I repent of my sin and ask forgiveness. I confess with my mouth Jesus as Lord and believe in my heart that God raised him from the dead. I accept you Lord Jesus as my Lord and Savior." The Bible says there is great joy in heaven whenever one person does this, and they are sealed in the Holy Spirit.

The last item covered with the inmates is the need to find a church when they have an opportunity. Finding a church necessitates discussing another essential Christian concept (that everyone seems to forget). The all-important concept is that there is no perfect church because, as soon as I enter it, it is no longer perfect. Churches are made up of other flawed people trying to lead the Christian life in community together. Most of the apostle Paul's letters were written to local congregations, demonstrating the local church's importance. In our individualistic culture, we tend to think we can go it alone, but that is not biblical. We all need to find a church that believes in the main doctrines of the Christian faith, teaches directly from the New and Old Testaments, and tries to live by the tenants of those teachings. The local congregation baptizes new believers and gives communion regularly.

This concludes some of the central tenets of Christian

salvation. If you rejected a "Christianity" that taught something different from these, then it should have been rejected. The true Christian faith is for anyone who knows they are not perfect and wants to accept God's love and grace through his Son to have a relationship with a loving God now and forever. Everyone is free to accept or reject the message.

Christianity is an exceptionally tolerant religion because we believe in a loving God. Forced belief violates the very definition of love. If you overpower someone with brute force and make them say they love you, this is not love. God cared so deeply for us; he did not make us robots. No matter what your worldview, my desire is that the reader can at least now understand some foundational principles of the largest religion in the world today. However, there are many other issues, questions, or misconceptions people have concerning Christianity that we need to address.

DOING WHAT YOU WANT TO DO

One of the most significant underlying issues people have with Christianity (even though they may not admit it) is that they don't like the idea of restrictions contrary to what they may want to do. No one likes constraints on their freedom. Is it possible, though, that what God takes away with one hand he gives back more abundantly with the other? Could it be that the few restrictions we do have are the ones that prevent us from destroying our lives and relationships? If there is a God, and if he is a good and rational God as the Bible says he is, then there is a pretty good chance he designed us for the ultimate purpose of being connected in a close friendship with Him. A relationship with God leads to healthy relationships with others. When we alienate ourselves from the One who created us, we fill the void with pornography, excessive alcohol, drugs, money, achieving the perfect look, the perfect social media persona, and many other things that always come up short. Instead of being free without God, we enslave ourselves to counterfeits that control us. The counterfeits can easily destroy our lives and the lives of our loved ones.

A free democratic society also requires restraints on behavior, or people's urges quickly infringe upon others' rights. When people voluntarily restrain their behavior and try to treat others as they would like to be treated, the entire nation benefits. The maximum amount of freedom occurs in a society when people are taking responsibility for their actions and have a desire to treat others well. All you have to do is look back on history to determine that people are not perfect. People are only safe and secure to do those things they would like to do when others are not allowed to harm and interfere with them. Therefore, freedom requires some restraint. The best kind of restraint is the kind people want to do because they know a loving and good God has laid out some rules for life for everyone's benefit. Instead of denying our freedom, the Christian worldview gives us the greatest amount of freedom, both individually and as a society, to exercise our gifts. It does this by giving us the desire and ability to follow guidelines that benefit our families and us. If this is true, we should be able to see if Christianity actually helped the world.

WHAT GOOD CAME FROM IT

Science is one good thing that came out of Christian belief. This catches people by surprise because of atheism, or secular humanism, teaching otherwise. Both Alfred North Whitehead and J. Robert Oppenheimer, neither a Christian, have stressed that modern science was born out of a Christian worldview.[2] The belief in a good and rational God leads to the belief that there is a rational world around us, and we are to go explore it and figure out how it works.

Francis Bacon, a Christian, is known as the father of the scientific method. He was a lawyer and a philosopher who had many talents, and he formally laid out the scientific method based on inquiry, observation, and experimentation. Some of the more famous scientists who were Christians include Blaise Pascal, Robert Boyle, Isaac Newton, Michael Faraday, Samuel Morse, Charles Babbage, Gregor Mendel, James Clerk Maxwell, George Washington Carver, Arthur Eddington, and Warner Heisenberg. Most of the Royal Society of London, in its early days, were almost all Christians. There were many others who were less famous and also many who may not have been public in their views but did operate from a Christian worldview perspective.

Christianity also birthed higher education by establishing the first two universities in the world in the middle of the 12th century, one in Paris and the other in Bologna. Oxford and Cambridge were founded around 1200, and many others soon followed all over Europe. By the early 13th century Paris, Bologna, Oxford, and Toulouse probably enrolled anywhere from several hundred to 1,500 students each.[3] The combination of an emphasis on higher education and the advent of the scientific method also gave Western civilization an advantage in providing some of the best hospitals and medical care in the world. Constantine the Great and St. Basil are credited with starting the first modern hospitals in the fourth century, but there has been a continuous increase in medical knowledge through the centuries motivated by Christian ethics and science.

The whole concept of human rights is another idea that emanated from a Christian worldview. The origin of the good things we have in our culture is often hidden to us because we live in the culture where they have existed for a long time, so we take them for granted. We can frequently gain some perspective through the observations of another person who has grown up in a different country and studies our own culture and history from an outsider's perspective.

I wrote parts of this book while staying in Mumbai, India. The differences in our history and customs are striking. While there, I just happened to read a book by an Indian intellectual, Vishal Mangalwadi. While still in his university studies at Allahabad, where he was born, Mangalwadi started questioning many of his beliefs. At the same time, he wondered about the source of many of the positive developments in his hometown over the last two hundred years. The positive developments were in the realms of higher education, hospitals, a free press, and greater political freedoms. After much study, he was astonished to discover that the Bible was the source of practically everything good in his hometown.[4] He found that the universities, hospitals, freedom of the press, and greater political freedoms originated, not from the British colonialists, but from the Christian missionaries who followed them. He brilliantly chronicled his research in *The Book That Made Your World*.

In the book, he tells how his wife, Ruth, meets the families in the village where they had just moved. She discovered that the youngest daughter of one of the families was starving to death. Ruth Mangalwadi tried to help the girl, named Sheela, and offered food and assistance to no avail. The parents starved the girl to death anyway because she was a burden to the family. They already had two sons and a daughter to babysit those sons, so another daughter was unnecessary. The price of another future dowry was too high, so her karma was to die.

Traditionally, there has not been much motivation in alleviating the suffering of the lower castes in India because to do so is to interfere with karma. What they did in a previous life determines the misery they have in this life. Sheela's parents and their neighbors did not understand why the Mangawaldi's wanted to save her life. It was the biblical view that inspired Ruth to try to save Sheela. The parents and the other villagers could not comprehend the Mangalwadis' compassion. Three thousand years of Hinduism, 2,600 years of Buddhism, 1,000 years of Islam, and a century of secularism had collectively failed to give them a convincing basis for affirming the value of a human being.[5]

Christianity says that all people are created in God's image. This changes everything as far as human rights are concerned. The end result embedded itself into the Declaration of Independence as the founders declared, "We hold these truths to be self-evident, that all men are created equal, that they are endowed by their Creator with certain unalienable rights, that among these are life, liberty, and the pursuit of happiness."

The foundation for democracy was laid in the 16th century when the Bible was finally printed, with the help of Gutenberg's printing press, in common European languages. The desire to understand the Bible greatly increased literacy and people discovered the hidden truths concerning man's true identity. Biblical literacy led to a yearning for greater religious freedom and the desire to go to the New World to escape Europe's state churches.

Like the pilgrims at Plymouth colony, many of the first colonists in America were seeking a place to worship freely. The only book many of these colonists owned was the Bible, and they wanted their families to know how to read it. A century and a half later, near the time of the American Revolution, the colonists were well aware that their creator had indeed endowed them with certain unalienable rights since we were created in God's image in Genesis Chapter 1. The concept of equality and greater literacy started to dismantle the class system brought from Europe as people were able to rise to different levels in society based on merit.

They also were very aware of the Bible's doctrine of the sinful nature of man. They were not that impressed, then, with King George III, likewise a sinful man, ruling over them without representation. These concepts were all well known to the framers of the US Constitution since the majority were Christians. Because we are all created in God's image, we are equal and should all have a vote. At the same time, man is by nature sinful, so we needed three equal branches of government to guard against one branch becoming powerful enough to take away our rights as citizens.

Secular humanist historians have tried to maintain that the Greeks brought us democracy as we know it. However, Greek democracies lasted at most a couple of decades. They then degenerated into mob rule because they were not based on man's equality as derived from being created in God's image. Plato hated democracy since he equated it to the mob rule that killed his mentor, Socrates. Plato believed in a philosopher-king who ruled with an iron hand. Plato's pupil, Aristotle, tutored Alexander the Great, who became the perfect example of the strong conquering king.[6] Greek thought ultimately brought us dictators, not democracy.

The Greeks and Romans also never gave a thought to ending

slavery because their societies depended on it. It took Christians to end slavery—not once, but twice. As an evangelical Christian and member of Parliament, William Wilberforce spearheaded the movement to end slavery in England in the early 1800s. Christians such as Charles Finney, Theodore Weld, Harriet Beecher Stowe, and Sojourner Truth led the abolitionist movement in the United States in the mid-1800s. Treating other races as inferior is abhorrent to true Christianity. God created only one race, the human race, and people have different levels of melanin in their skin. If you really think about it, Jesus abolished slavery almost 2,000 years ago when he commanded his followers to love your neighbor as yourself.

The Christian worldview is the very source of the human rights that we take for granted. It has birthed modern science, higher education, medical advancements, abolitionist movements, and paved the way for modern democracies. It gave us the basis of our laws that provided the framework for the freest and most prosperous country in the world.

BUT WHAT ABOUT THE CRUSADES AND THE SPANISH INQUISITION

Has not Christianity also caused a lot of bad things? There is no doubt that there have been some terrible things committed in the name of Christianity. We should ask two questions, though. Were the people committing the offenses doing exactly what Jesus says not to do? If someone steals your Social Security number and identity and commits securities and banking fraud, are you guilty? Many people have stolen Jesus's identity and committed crimes in his name. The second question you should ask is whether a country or ruler hijacked Christianity to achieve a ruler's or nation-state's goals?

Concerning the Crusades, vast numbers of people today either have not been taught or do not remember basic history. After Mohammed died in 632, Islam spread swiftly by the sword for 100 years. Finally, Charles "The Hammer" Martel stopped Islam's advance at the Battle of Tours, France in 732. Christianity fought a defensive war with Islam for 450 years before the first Crusade in 1095. The Crusades were primarily a defensive response to Islamic military expansion.[7] Both sides committed atrocities. Christians are clearly allowed to defend themselves in a sinful world, but the New Testament never says to spread Christianity with the sword. Christianity has spread tremendously during persecution and the sword being used on it. On the other hand, Islam has spread the fastest using the sword on others and is a definite part of what Mohammed modeled.

The Spanish Inquisition is probably the next most common injustice brought up when discussing Christianity. The Inquisition was a tribunal or court set up by Spanish monarchs Ferdinand and Isabella in 1478 to maintain Catholic orthodoxy in their kingdoms. The tribunals lasted about 350 years. The Spanish Inquisition sentenced approximately 3,000 people to death. This is another explicit example of rulers doing what the New Testament says not to do since Jesus never advocated compulsion. People should also know, however, that Spain had many enemies at the time. The Dutch and English propagated numerous extreme exaggerations concerning the Inquisition for political purposes. New historians have gained full access to the complete archives of the inquisitions. This knowledge, combined with researching diaries, letters, and other old documents, have demonstrated that the tribunals were much fairer than the secular courts spread across Europe at the time.[8] We gain perspective when one considers King Henry VIII of England may have ordered the execution of somewhere between 57,000 and 72,000 people.

The Thirty Years' War is another example often mentioned regarding religion causing the death of many people. When you study the conflict, however, you find rulers hijacking Christianity for political and geographical gain. Translators did not produce Bibles in common European languages until the 16th century, and it took quite a while for people to comprehend what was in there. The people were not able to hold monarchs and governments accountable for years to come.

There is no doubt imperfect people have committed some terrible acts in the name of Christianity. Also, there are people who say they are Christians who are not. Jesus tells his followers his most important parable is the parable of the sower. Seed is sown on the road and birds steal it. More seed is thrown on stony ground and does not develop roots. Other seeds are choked out by weeds representing the cares of this world. Finally, some seed is sown on the good soil (of a repentant heart).

In the very next parable Jesus tells his disciples there are certain tares (weeds) that look like wheat. If we try to remove the tares, we might also remove the wheat. Jesus goes on to say, though, we will know them by their fruit. False conversions can occur when people say they are Christians strictly for cultural or family reasons; or, perhaps, they are told Christianity will make their life better. They sign on without looking at their own sinful condition and the need for repentance. Eventually, one can tell something is wrong if there is no change in how they conduct their life. Christians should not doubt their salvation, but if there is no change in your life and actions, then revisit repentance.

Christians are not perfect, but one should see a change in their life that eventually bears fruit.

Atheists and secular humanists like to say that religion has caused most wars and most suffering. I say this is categorically false. Christianity has done tremendous good in the world. We should never forget that atheism killed up to 100 million people in the 20th century. Hitler, Stalin, Mao, and Pol Pot combined killed close to this number; and they killed mostly citizens of the countries they ruled. The numbers are so staggering we can hardly comprehend this level of evil.

WHAT ABOUT EVIL, SUFFERING, AND HELL?

Another common argument against Christianity is that a loving God would not allow evil, suffering, or hell. While addressing this issue, I ask that the reader keep a question in the back of their mind. The question is, "Is it possible that the God who exploded this universe, up to 100 billion trillion stars, into perfect order out of nothing and created the incredible complexity of life, could have a different opinion or viewpoint than myself?" I ask this to provide a reminder that there may be some things going on that we don't totally comprehend. At the same time, evil and suffering are very legitimate concerns to bring up.

The critic may say the Christian God has left the world a mess with pain-and-suffering beyond belief. Your omnipotent God is either not smart enough, powerful enough, or he just does not care. These are the only three options. Which is it? But these are not the only three options. The fourth option is that God has an excellent reason, and we do not know what it is because we do not know all things.[9] CIPA is a rare condition that does not allow a person to feel pain. People with CIPA can burn themselves or hurt themselves in various ways without knowing it. Parents of children with this condition desperately want their children to feel pain so as not to destroy their bodies.[10] Perhaps pain allows us to have freedom of movement in this world without continually injuring ourselves.

Also, is it possible that character and virtues develop most fully in a world such as ours? Could we learn courage and fortitude in a world where nothing happens to us? How do we know what evil is? How do you know if the line is crooked unless you know what a straight line looks like?[11] Evil and suffering are terrible challenges, and God has given us something to do. He expects us to go out and do something about them. The problem of evil and suffering often involves a person thinking to themselves, "If I were God, I would have done it differently." We live in a democratic society, and subconsciously believe we should have a vote. A person from China once told a pastor in our country that people in China understand that God certainly has every right to conduct the world according to his perfect purpose.[12] We are not God and do not see the whole picture. He will do away with evil and suffering eventually, but only in his timing.

The idea of hell also evokes strong emotions. People cannot believe that a loving God would create such a place. But God is also a holy God, which means sin cannot be allowed in his presence. Someone who thinks they should be allowed in God's presence in their present condition is similar to someone thinking they should be able to walk on the sun's surface. The heat would vaporize them. A perfect and holy God is without sin or blemish and cannot allow sinful humanity into his presence until addressing the sin problem. Christ died on the cross for all of humankind's sins, but it is appropriated by faith. If someone chooses against God, then that person is selecting their final destination. That is why some people will say hell is actually locked from the inside. The rational response is for a person to choose Christ, so they know their final destination and then help as many other people to accept Christ as well. Perhaps a person's pride is potentially so immense that some people would rather risk eternity in hell than humble themselves and repent.

ERRORS IN THE BIBLE

In the previous chapter, we already validated the Old Testament's incredible accuracy based on the discovery and analysis of the Dead Sea Scrolls. But what about the New Testament? Are there not a lot of errors and problems with it? We have hundreds of manuscripts and fragments of manuscripts of the New Testament that date back to the first four centuries after Christ. If you include later centuries as well, we have thousands of New Testament manuscripts. The New Testament has earlier manuscripts, more manuscripts, and more abundantly supported manuscripts than the best ten pieces of classical literature combined.[13] Opponents have complained the only reason for the tremendous textual support is because the religion originated in an arid climate. Complain if you want to, the main point is that the New Testament has enormous documentary support.

If you reject the Bible because there are errors in the numerous manuscripts, you would also have to reject the writings of Plato, Herodotus, Euripides, Aristotle, and Homer.[14] All ancient written works emanate from later manuscripts or parts of manuscripts because the originals have not survived. Because of the academic discipline known as textual criticism, we can trace scribal errors and additions by comparing them to the earliest manuscripts—the more documents available from different times and places, the more likely one can find mistakes. Because we have so many copies of the New Testament, some recent scholars have claimed massive numbers of errors exist. They make this claim by counting every little scribal error in every manuscript. The vast majority of these errors are due to punctuation and spelling. This practice is deeply deceptive since we can trace back to where the first errors occurred and thus determine what the original should say very accurately.

I know this is unnerving for some people to think that there could be errors in these manuscripts, even if they are minor ones. However, I maintain that God knew what he was doing. If the originals existed and fell into the hands of an Emperor or dictator, they could change the original and alter entire doctrines in the process. With numerous manuscripts springing up all over the Roman Empire, any scribal error due to poor lighting or additions due to misguided enthusiasm is uncovered. Distinguished Princeton textual critic Bruce Metzger estimated the New Testament is 99.5% accurate.[15] The five words out of a thousand in doubt are usually of the form *us* versus *we*, and there is no Christian doctrine affected in the least.[16] One could easily say this level of accuracy in an ancient document is a miracle.

WEREN'T THE STORIES JUST MADE UP?

The problem with thinking the witnesses made up the stories is that they had nothing to gain in doing so. They were already members of a monotheistic religion, Judaism, and proclaiming a Messiah only brought persecution and horrific deaths to the disciples. They were eyewitnesses to everything Jesus said and did. They could have escaped crucifixion, beheading, and other violent deaths by merely denying the events. They never did. There is a vast difference between someone being brainwashed with something they never saw and ultimately flying airplanes into skyscrapers, and people who were actual eyewitnesses and yet would not recant under terrible persecution.

Simon Greenleaf was an influential lawyer and jurist who was instrumental in starting Harvard Law school. He was an expert in testimony and set out to see if the testimony contained in the four Gospels would stand up in a 19th-century court of law in the United States. He found that the testimony would indeed stand up remarkably well. The witnesses told the same story from different perspectives, noticing various details. This is known as divergent testimony and is very powerful. The testimony that does not hold up is from witnesses who tell the exact same story verbatim—every little detail reported the same way. These are the made-up stories. The early disciples included different details in their descriptions, reflecting varied professions and perspectives of the witness but always telling the same overall story. The New Testament witnesses also included embarrassing information about themselves and difficult statements by Jesus. They also included a multitude of easily verifiable facts. They tell you the time, place, names, and other specifics. Historically, these have all been backed up extraordinarily well by other sources.

Josh McDowell was a skeptic and in a university wanting to pursue a law degree. Some Christians he met challenged him to look at the evidence for the truth of the New Testament. McDowell took up the challenge and vigorously set out to disprove the claims of Christianity. After looking at the evidence, he became a Christian himself. He describes the experience:

I left the University and traveled throughout the United States and Europe to gather evidence to prove that Christianity is a sham.

One day while I was sitting in a library in London, England, I sensed a voice within me saying, "Josh, you don't have a leg to stand on." I immediately suppressed it. But just about every day after that I heard the same inner voice. The more I researched, the more I heard this voice. I returned to the United States and to the University, but couldn't sleep at night. I would go to bed at 10 o'clock and lie awake until four in the morning trying to refute the overwhelming evidence I was accumulating that Jesus Christ was God's son.[17]

He eventually accepted the evidence and went on to write several books detailing that evidence.

Lee Strobel was a graduate of Yale Law School and employed as the *Chicago Tribune* legal affairs editor. He was shocked when he found out that his wife had become a Christian. He was an atheist and set out to use all his law and journalism training to prove Christianity false. Like Josh McDowell, he also came to an opposite conclusion:

Setting aside my self-interest and prejudices as best I could, I read books, interviewed experts, asked questions, analyzed history, explored archaeology, studied ancient literature, and for the first time in my life picked apart the Bible verse by verse.

I plunged into the case with more vigor than with any story I had ever pursued. I applied the training I had received at Yale Law School as well as my experience as legal affairs editor of the *Chicago Tribune*. And over time the evidence of the world—of history, of science, of philosophy, of psychology–began to point toward the unthinkable.[18]

Lee Strobel eventually became a Christian. He told his story and chronicled his research in several books and became a *New York Times* best-selling author. Both Josh McDowell and Lee Strobel are great examples of what can happen if people will actually take the time to examine the historical data concerning Christianity.

C. S. Lewis taught at both Oxford and Cambridge and was one of the greatest literary geniuses and writers of the 20th century. He was an atheist who was also willing to examine Christianity both philosophically and historically. The most significant stumbling block preventing him from believing in God was the problem of evil. The change came for him when he finally asked himself how he knew what evil was:

My argument against God was that the universe seemed so cruel and unjust. But how had I got this idea of just and unjust? A man does not call a line crooked unless he has some idea of a straight line. What was I comparing this universe with when I called it unjust? If the whole show was bad and senseless from A to Z, so to speak, why did I, who was supposed to be part of the show, find myself in such a violent reaction against it? A man feels wet when he falls in the water, because man is not a water animal: a fish would not feel wet. Of course I could have given up my idea of justice by saying it was nothing but a private idea of my own. But if I did that, then my argument against God collapsed too—for the argument depended on saying that the world was really unjust, not simply that it did not happen to please my private fantasies. Thus in the very act of trying to prove that God did not exist—in other words, that the whole of reality was senseless—I found I was forced to assume that one part of reality—namely my idea of justice—was full of sense. Consequently atheism turns out to be too simple. If the whole universe has no meaning, we should never have found out that it has no meaning: just as, if there were no light in the universe and therefore no creatures with eyes, we should never know it was dark. Dark would be without meaning.[19]

C. S. Lewis became a Christian at age 32. If we are intellectually and philosophically honest, we can come to some conclusions that may truly surprise us.

MIRACLES

Some people like to say that miracles are impossible. One could say miracles cannot occur if there is absolute proof there is no God, but there is no airtight argument disproving the existence of God. In fact, over the last 25 years, the airtight evidence seems to point massively to God's existence. If God exists, then miracles are possible.[20] An all-powerful God certainly can momentarily interrupt the normal physical forces to accomplish his purposes.[21] Interestingly, as we have seen in previous chapters, the two greatest miracles surround us at all times—the creation of the universe and first life (not to mention advanced life and

the human brain). The atheist worldview has recently perme-
ated our universities and other bastions of influence. Secularism
constantly bombards our culture with purely atheist viewpoints.
Thus, miracles might not seem possible until you look closely at
the universe and its creation and the complexity of life around
you.

Another common argument against the Bible's truth and
infallibility is grounded in the fact that men wrote it. Again,
statements like this presuppose that an all-powerful God does
not exist. If students can sit in class and write down notes from
a teacher, then men chosen by God can certainly write down
his communicated thoughts. One of the primary characteristics
of an intelligent agent is the ability to communicate. It almost
seems absurd that a being capable of creating the universe could
not communicate with us as he desires.

I could go on ad infinitum addressing the objections people have towards Christianity, but time and space allow only
so much. Nonetheless, I have covered a good number of them
because of the amount of misinformation or incomplete information put out over the Internet in the last couple of decades.
Skeptics and antagonists have probably scrutinized the New
Testament more than any other document in the history of the
world.[22] One of the things the Christian worldview has in its
favor is that it has been under attack for 2,000 years and has
weathered the inspection extremely well.

LOOKING BACK

As we look back at the previous chapters, I made a case for certain
behaviors, actions, and attitudes leading to better life outcomes

both individually and collectively. But what are they grounded
in other than my own opinion and the sources I quote? Over
the last several thousand years, history records the never-ending
philosophic views of men. One philosopher gives the unified and
true knowledge of what reality is, then the next one says no and
scratches it out and offers his view. Then another comes along,
scratches that out, and gives another perspective. Then another
scratches that out and states a different opinion. Again and again,
this goes on through the centuries.[23] Philosopher Allan Bloom
summarizes Friedrich Nietzsche:

> Values are not discovered by reason, and it is fruitless to
> seek them, to find the truth of the good life. The quest
> begun by Odysseus and continued over three millen-
> nia has come to an end with the observation that there
> is nothing to seek. This alleged fact was announced by
> Nietzsche just over a century ago when he said, "God
> is dead." Good and evil now for the first time appeared
> as values, of which there have been a thousand and one,
> none rationally or objectively preferable to any other...
> In short, Nietzsche with the utmost gravity told modern
> man that he was free falling in the abyss of nihilism.[24]

Values have to be grounded in something more than opinions.
For instance, it is a bit disjointed to say that we all evolved from
pond scum, therefore, go out and live a life of beauty, value, and
loving others.

Perhaps like Vishal Mangalwadi, mentioned earlier in this
chapter, I am also a little surprised that Christianity is the hidden
force behind almost all of the values drawn out previously in
this book. I started off in Chapter 1 by discussing the concept of

success and mentioning three core elements. The first one was family and relationships. The Bible begins with a marriage and ends with a marriage and is a word picture for God's reconciling work to the world. He cares deeply about family, children, and relationships because he created them, and He is relational himself. The second element was work. Work is extremely important to us because God worked in his creation event and continues to work. He made us in his image, so we are designed for creative work. The last element was treating others as we would like to be treated ourselves. Jesus summed up the entire Ten Commandments in just two. Love the Lord your God with all your heart, all your mind, all your soul, and all your strength; and love others as you love yourself. That second part is all about treating others as you would like to be treated yourself. Christians would add another element to success–to have faith in Christ, which allows you to fulfill the purposes God has for you and to have the assurance of eternal life.

Next in Chapter 2, we discussed relationships in greater detail. The Bible also has a lot to say specifically about our relationships. Much of what I brought out points to God's guidelines that he has given us in the Bible to help us not destroy our family and other friendships. Again, what God takes away with one hand, he gives back more abundantly with the other.

In Chapter 3, the section on personal finances, much of what was laid out can be found in the book of Proverbs. There is a consistent warning in the Bible about indebtedness and the debtor being a slave to the lender. There is also mention of diversifying one's investments to avoid taking excessive risk in just one area.

In the realm of politics as discussed in Chapter 4, much of the essence is derived from the Christian concept that man is by nature sinful. Political and economic systems that have a utopian view of man have always ended in disaster. At the same time, Christianity teaches we are created in God's image and gives us the basis of our human rights that guarantees our freedoms of speech, religion, press, petition, and assembly. We are to treat one another in our private and public debates with gentleness and respect to not trample on these rights. We are also to help others who are in genuine need, both locally and around the world. The Bible has a lot to say about helping the poor, widows, and orphans.

Chapter 5's discussion on higher education was primarily about the concept of truth. We are reasoning creatures, and reason itself points to logic, objective standards, design, and truth. The Christian God is also a God of logic, reason, and design. He is also the ultimate standard, and he states that his word is truth. If there is truth, then there is truth in morality as well. God has given us moral principles to protect us and society as a whole.

Every community has beliefs or truth claims that exclude others. In essence, every group is exclusive—or it's not a group—it's just everybody. Like any group or community, Christianity also has its beliefs and standards of behavior, but at the same time is very inclusive of imperfect people. Christian belief should also lead its members to treat persons in other communities with love and respect, and to serve them and meet their needs.[25]

In summation, Christianity is different from what a lot of people think it is. When we carefully examine Christian faith and find out what it truly is, we find it hidden behind many cherished values. Whether Christian or not, the reader should know some details about the world's largest religion to understand the world around them. Every worldview needs to account for the five great questions of origin, identity, meaning, morality, and destiny. A great generation will know what they truly believe, to have the conviction to passionately engage the world around them.

9

CONCLUSIONS

Looking Ahead

CLICKBAIT! GET THE SOUNDBITE. YOU know how it works. We all have done it at some time or another. You are browsing along looking for something appealing, and then you see a headline that grabs you. You tap or click on it and read an article that is hopefully not too long. If the news article or editorial touches upon politics or worldview, you are especially looking for a nice, short soundbite or two you can remember that reinforces what you already believe. The intriguing article subconsciously builds upon your confirmation bias and gives you a pleasant feeling deep down inside. Every once in a while, you click on a caption you think will reinforce what you believe, but something unexpected happens. The article goes in the opposite direction, and you flee, exiting the site as fast as possible. You start browsing anew, looking for something a little safer.

We live in a clickbait, soundbite world. Media outlets are competing with one another using attention engineers and marketing geniuses to get you to click on their articles or sites. News organizations used to be able to maintain some level of objectivity and still make a profit enabling them to stay in business. Today, though, there is so much competition, media companies throw objectivity out the window. News outlets know who their target audience is, and they serve up what that audience wants, or they could lose them. Young journalists almost have no choice but to follow the dictates of their employer. Many print newspapers have, for the most part, shut down. If a young employed journalist does not toe the line, he or she will end up unemployed in a bleak landscape. Welcome to the world of polarization.

Because we may believe certain things for psychological reasons (it gives comfort or justifies us in some way) and sociological reasons (our friends, family, and people we admire believe the same thing), we unwittingly contribute to polarization when we only click on the header we might like. Then add to this mix the phenomenon that people have tried to redefine tolerance as meaning you have to agree with them, and we have a severe problem. We used to call this narrowmindedness, referring to someone who did not read broadly to gain a wide spectrum of knowledge. I think a lot of educated people today might be surprised and offended if you pointed out that they are actually very narrow-minded when they get all their information from sources that give only one perspective.

These educated people would be surprised because they consider themselves open-minded and tolerant of everything. Remember, though, we all look at the world through a grid (almost like a sieve) of presuppositions of what we believe is true about what exists. Those presuppositions allow us to hold on to some information and let other things go. Total open-mindedness causes us not to hold on to anything and leads to a rather vacuous state of mind. It is ironic that the very people who consider themselves the most open-minded are actually some of the most narrow-minded. If someone states that they are totally open and tolerant of everything while they hold firmly to a very narrow position, consider asking them what books they have read representing the opposing view and what were some of the arguments, pro and con, of that view. Encountering their complete silence is a strong possibility.

We want to be open-minded in the inquiry phase and the research phase of assimilating information. Still, eventually, we should accept things as true based on the coherence, consistency, and completeness of the facts and evidence. Evaluating information in this manner is known as developing a presupposition philosophically and is superior to believing things only for sociological and psychological reasons.[1]

You may notice that people who are not afraid to read or view information from both sides, and then think it through, are not easily threatened during a discussion. They are usually the ones who can stay reasonably calm during a debate. We would all help ourselves immensely if we would intentionally read news articles and editorials and watch news programs that represent both sides of the political debate. If you do this, you will immediately notice how much bias is displayed by what an outlet chooses not to cover. You simply won't know about significant news occurrences if you look at only one political perspective since media organizations refuse to report events they do not find advantageous. Always remember, even if an organization is biased, its journalists can still convey some factual circumstances. They just may exhibit a particular slant.

BOOKS

We can also help ourselves going forward as a society if we choose to read books. Even studying just one serious book every year or two could massively improve the current situation. Younger generations should not get discouraged if they cannot read prolifically during the busy phases of life. However, one should strive to read something of an enlightening nature sometime during the year. Abraham Lincoln was defined, not by how many books he read, but by how well he knew the books he did read.

As is often the case, my wife had a huge impact on me several years ago when she asked a simple question. She knew I had just finished a nonfiction book a few days prior. She does not like to miss out on anything, so she naturally asked me, "What was the book about?" After thinking for a moment, my perplexed look said it all. I could not tell her one major point of the book even though I had just finished reading it a few days before. What was even worse was that she had asked me a similar question about a different book a few months earlier, and I think I gave her the same answer. There was something clearly wrong. I decided at the time to do something different in the future. I resolved to write something down summarizing a few of the main points of any subsequent book I might read. I have held to that for a decade, and the notes from the better books are substantial.

I travel extensively and don't watch a great deal of TV (except, of course, for certain football games and favorite Pro soccer), so I have a little more time on the road than most people. Even if you do not have a lot of time, it is still easy to write down a few of the main points from anything you may have underlined or annotated in some way. I have joked a few times with people that I prefer paper copies of good books because the battery life is phenomenal, and the handwriting recognition software is to die for. My notes, scribbles, and underlining never change with any new version. In reality, I think I like books printed on real paper because I just get tired of looking at screens all day. When I review my notes from the books I have read, I have found that I routinely come to material where I could swear I had never read the information before in my life. Even though I took notes from the precise words, the material appeared entirely new upon review. We have to reread notes a few times before they stick in our memory.

I have said before that life is a gift and an adventure and should be lived accordingly. With that in mind, this whole book thing might sound kind of tedious. But here is the deal. There are life situations where ten hours of reading a book can save you ten years or more of dealing with some massive problem. You could have avoided or successfully solved the problem if you had the knowledge; however, you do not have the knowledge if you do not remember it. Some areas of life this truly applies to are marriage, raising children, business and financial skills, and life values. I encourage everyone to read some good books and write down some of the main points so you can review them later. Building wisdom in this way is one of those habits that can change your life.

Reading books can also help people in a few other ways. You develop critical thinking skills more readily when you follow the logical arguments of an author to completion. The click-bait-soundbite world can rob us of the ability to think logically through an issue or debate. We get used to getting fast, short segments that build on our confirmation bias and short-circuit critical thinking. Authors may also expose us to viewpoints and information we would not generally come upon, which gives us a broader perspective. We might not necessarily agree with the author on some points, but a wise person learns to put certain concepts or information up on a mental shelf for the moment and get back to them later. In hindsight, I have learned many good things from authors that held different opinions than my own.

IS HISTORY BORING?

There is a law at work in the world that economists and some social scientists are keenly aware of, but the average person is not cognizant. The law is known as the law of unintended consequences. The law refers to the fact that there are frequently unforeseen outcomes from proposed actions or policies. The unexpected outcomes are sometimes positive, but way too often, they harm individuals or entire societies. We have already covered the positive effects of people allowing market conditions to set prices. Then democracies allow people to work freely producing goods and services as well as participating in their consumption. The unintended positive consequences include people willingly serving one another and the extremely efficient production of what is needed. An unintended negative consequence covered earlier was Marxism destroying incentive. Marxism also causes an extremely inefficient distribution of goods and services, leaving countries impoverished. Utopian systems always lead to unintended harmful consequences because they do not account for people's real behavior. They bring disaster for the average person and create "utopia" (dictatorial power) only for the leaders.

But there are many more unforeseen outcomes lurking in the world around us. How do we even know where to look for them in the realm of government actions and policies? This is where a knowledge of history looms large. As they say, people who do not know history are doomed to repeat it. I realize the younger a person is, the less relevant history appears to them. I assure you, the older you get, the more interesting history becomes as it plays out before your eyes. An educated person can think critically in diverse fields, and the field of history is one area every person needs to take seriously.

Another reason you should read good history books is to undo all the harm done by historians like Howard Zinn. Zinn seemed to have a free pass for several decades to write almost anything he wanted without generating much academic criticism. Today, it is fairly common knowledge that he described himself as somewhat of a Marxist and anarchist. He was an extremely biased, if not fraudulent, historian. Dr. Sam Wineburg, the Margaret Jack's Professor of Education at Stanford University and Director of the Stanford History Education Group, has criticized Zinn extensively in an essay and in his book. The *Stanford News* reported:

> Wineburg, one of the world's top researchers in the field of history education, raises larger issues about how history should be taught. He says that Zinn's desire to cast a light on what he saw as historic injustice was a crusade built on secondary sources of questionable provenance, omission of exculpatory evidence, leading questions and shaky connections between evidence and conclusions.[2]

In his 2018 book *Why Learn History (When It's Already on Your Phone)*, Dr. Wineberg devotes all of chapter 3 to exposing and meticulously documenting exactly how Zinn misled his readers in *A People's History of the United States*. Common examples include making generalizations about nearly 13 million black citizens by citing three anecdotes, while at the same time ignoring about 2,427,495 eligible black registrants. The number of conscientious objectors was significantly lower than Zinn hypothesized, and most served very honorably.[3]

Zinn also made sure he did not mention the Nazi's Operation Wasserkante, the decimation of Warsaw on September 25, 1939. Hitler's goal was to terrorize and to eliminate living forces. Forty thousand Poles perished. Numerous Polish Jews were herded into the forest and mowed down before open pits. Zinn instead focuses on lesser Nazi attacks on Coventry and Rotterdam to make the allies' attacks look worse than what the Nazis were doing.[4]

Howard Zinn tries to make the use of the atomic bomb appear completely unnecessary. He bases his argument on an intercepted cable sent by the Japanese Foreign Minister to his ambassador in Moscow on July 12, 1945. No such cable exists. He totally ignored documents that have come to light since Emperor Hirohito's death. Zinn tries to make the Rosenbergs and the Communist Party of the United States of America appear wholly innocent. Again, he ignores all the archives unlocked after Boris Yeltsin became Russia's president.[5]

Sam Wineburg's credentials are impeccable. We owe him a debt of gratitude because few people can comprehend the amount of damage done by the fraudulent history written by Howard Zinn. Much of what is going on in our streets can be attributed to a misleading history book whose aim was to make the United States, Western civilization, democracy, and the free enterprise system look bad in every historical situation. What is even more alarming is that much of academia was complicit in accepting such an obviously faulty and biased book.

History will include the good, the bad, and the indifferent, but historians do not get to make up stuff and interpret the writings any way they desire. When doing research, competent historians use several different tests to determine the reliability of a source. They may use a bibliographical test to judge how reliable the actual document or copy is. An external evidence test examines other historical material to confirm or deny the accuracy of the document. An internal evidence test determines whether the written testimony in the text itself is credible and to what extent. As part of the internal evidence test, the critic still must follow Aristotle's dictum. "The benefit of the doubt is to be given to the document itself, and not arrogated by the critic to himself."[6] Recent historians seem to think they can follow post-modernism's false premise of interpreting historical documents any way they wish. We must always guard ourselves against faulty research. The next great generation will read history written by credible historians who do not have an ideological ax to grind. In doing so, there is a good chance we can avoid many of the unintended consequences derived from faulty government policy that can destroy a nation.

THE FUTURE OF EDUCATION

Our discussion of history points to education or lack thereof. Faulty and extremely biased history taught in our schools and universities has contributed appallingly to our nation's societal breakdown. However, it is not just history, our measured academic performance in many subjects is dismal in cities and other areas across the nation. This is in spite of the fact that we have many dedicated teachers in our country. So what's going on?

The Project Baltimore Investigation into Baltimore's City School System sheds light on many of the problems. A few years

ago, in an editorial in The Hill, Armstrong Williams summarized
the results of the investigation:

...Baltimore spends roughly $1.4 billion annually on
education, or roughly $16,000 per student. Baltimore's
spending on education is the fourth highest of any mu-
nicipality in the country. Despite this massive commitment of resources, Baltimore schools have some of the
lowest educational proficiency levels in the country.

According to Project Baltimore investigative journalist
Chris Papst, reading proficiency rates among Baltimore
High School graduates hovered at around 11%, and math
proficiency rates hover around 12%. This is in a school
system that graduates roughly 70% of its students each
year. There is clearly a major disconnection between the
high graduation rate and the extremely dismal academic
proficiency rate.

This discrepancy alone, given the money that goes
into the system, is prima facie evidence of a crime.
As Project Baltimore continues to follow the path of
the money, it becomes increasingly obvious that there
are strong institutional incentives to keep Baltimore's
clearly failing system in place. In a very real sense,
the dysfunction in Baltimore's schools mirrors a similar dysfunction in the city's political establishment. In
a city of fewer than 600,000 residents, with a rapidly
declining school enrollment, literally thousands of individuals in the school system receive salaries in ex-
cess of $100,000 per year. Most of the recipients of this

government largess are not teachers but consultants, contractors, and administrators.

The school system, it seems, has become a platform for political patronage, and rewarding allies of the city's political class. How else could the school system's budget be so saddled with bureaucracy and blight?[7]

Reports like this should break our hearts. The destroyed futures of so many young men and women is an immense tragedy. What would happen if we duplicated Project Baltimore's investigation in low-performing city schools nationwide? I think we all know what we would find. The Baltimore school system's dismal performance is the expected result of a government-run monopoly controlled by union lobbying and political patronage. As the late Albert Shanker, head of the United Federation of Teachers, was honest enough to say years ago, "When schoolchildren start paying union dues, that's when I'll start representing the interests of schoolchildren."[8]

But would breaking up the public school monopoly and bringing in competition change anything? The Center for Research on Education Outcomes (CREDO) at Stanford University published its Urban Charter School Study Report on 41 Regions 2015. The research shows competition makes a huge difference. The report reveals that urban charter schools in the aggregate provide significantly higher annual growth levels in both math and reading than their TPS (traditional public schools) peers. When learning gains for urban charter students are presented for individual urban regions, regions with larger learning gains in charter schools outnumber those with smaller learning gains two-to-one. Learning gains for charter school students are more

substantial by significant amounts for Black, Hispanic, low income, and special education students in both math and reading.
Positive results for charter school students increased on average
over the period of the study. Compared to the charter school
landscape as a whole, the 41 urban charter regions have im-
proved results at both ends of the quality spectrum. Not every
charter school outperformed every public school because there
were vast differences in accountability and the way the charter
schools operated in different regions. The results were extremely
conclusive that overall, charter schools did far better in the 41
urban regions.[9] So how did we end up with this underperforming
education monopoly?

The 1947 Supreme Court decision, *Everson v. Board Of
Education*, laid the foundation for the current monopoly in public education. In a 5-4 decision, the Supreme Court sided with
Arch Everson, the plaintiff, whose complaint centered on the
fact that his school district used taxpayer funds to reimburse students attending private religious schools. They maintained this
constituted support for religion in violation of the due process
clause. The majority opinion stated the Constitution intended to
erect a "wall of separation" between Church and State.

The problem is the Constitution and the Bill of Rights say
nothing about a "wall of separation" between church and state.
The only mention of religion in the Constitution is that "no religious Test shall ever be required as a qualification to any Office
or public trust under the United States." The First Amendment
of the Bill of Rights only says, "Congress shall make no law
respecting an establishment of religion, or prohibiting the free
exercise thereof." At the time the Constitution and Bill of Rights
were written, many European countries had state religions.
Many of the early colonists fled the Church of England, so very

understandably, the framers wanted to make sure there would never be a Church of the United States.

The "wall of separation" between church and state language comes from a single personal letter written by Thomas Jefferson. Jefferson was not even at the Constitutional Convention in 1789 nor present for the drafting of the Bill of Rights. He wrote the letter in 1802 to the Danbury Baptist Association of Connecticut:

> "Believing with you that religion is a matter which lies solely between Man and his God, that he owes account to none other for his faith or worship, that the legitimate powers of government reach actions only, and not opinions, I contemplate with sovereign reverence the act of the whole American people which declared that their legislature should 'make no law respecting an establishment of religion, or prohibiting the free exercise thereof,' thus building a wall of separation between Church and State."

Jefferson's point was to highlight his agreement that Connecticut should not effectively establish the Congregationalist church as the Church of Connecticut. He then concluded his letter by asking for their "kind prayers for the protection and blessing of the common father and creator of man."

It is almost hard to believe the Supreme Court used a phrase from a president's personal letter to overthrow 160 years of constitutional law. In the private letter, again, the separation between church and state was only about a state, or the nation, establishing a monopoly religion or denomination. On the Internet you can find "wall of separation" wording in the Treaty of Tripoli falsely attributed to a nonexistent letter by George Washington.

No such letter has ever been found. There is also a bogus quotation from a letter Jefferson wrote to a group of Baptists in Virginia in 1808. The paragraph quoted is actually commentary from an editor and not from Jefferson himself.[10] In summary, the 1947 Supreme Court, in a narrow decision, dictated a wall of separation between church and state because the Supreme Court said so.

We should be thankful that our Constitution and Bill of Rights give us religious freedom and ensure there will never be a monopoly Church of the United States. However, the founders' intent was never to squelch all religious expression and symbols in the public sphere. Even a cursory look at the actions of the founding fathers will tell you that. Congress established the first congressional chaplain on May 1, 1789, and they opened the sessions in prayer. Their praying before meetings, among many other actions, reveals much about Congresses' intentions concerning religion.

The 1947 Everson v. Board of Education decision essentially established atheism as the only religion your tax dollars can fund. Yes, you read the sentence correctly. As we have already seen, atheism is faith-based. It also is a system of beliefs that gives meaning to the life of its adherents. That is what all religions do, and they do not need to invoke God to do so. Humanists and atheists even have chaplains at several college campuses. Buddhism, Confucianism, Shintoism, Jainism, and some other religions do not require God either. They are all worldviews that give meaning to those who adhere to their beliefs. Because atheism has disguised itself as a non-religion, when it really isn't, it has stealthily inserted itself as the only worldview legally authorized in taxpayer-funded schools.

There is no such thing as valueless education. I can assure

you there are some values taught in our secular public school curriculums, and the values often totally contradict the moral values of their parents. Sex education training for very young students is more like brainwashing. Parents of today's public school children need to see for themselves what values their school's curriculum promotes. Few parents would approve of the socialism promoted in the 1619 Project curriculum. The teaching of no morals or values eventually tells students there are no morals or values. The current secular public school monopoly is preparing our kids to become nihilists by the time they finish college.

We should all enthusiastically endorse the freedom of atheist parents to send their kids to atheist, secular schools with their tax dollars if they so desire. We should not endorse the rest of us, who have a different worldview, having to send our kids to the same schools to learn values that we find highly objectionable. I would never want children of atheist parents sent only to Christian schools against their will. Simple economics forces religious parents to send their children to secular atheist schools against their will. The majority of parents in our country cannot afford private schools, and so they have no choice but to send their children to the public school monopoly. The leaders who wrote our Constitution and Bill of Rights would be horrified to see the current situation that dictates tax dollars can only go to schools that teach from an atheist worldview centered curriculum.

So how did we ever end up with school systems that graduate students with an 11% proficiency in reading and 12% proficiency in math? How did we end up with universities that teach extremely distorted and biased views of history? You have to look no further than the current public school monopoly. Parents desperately need the freedom to choose charter schools, religious schools, or public schools with their tax dollars. Not only will you end up with much higher academic standards, but society will also benefit from students who are exposed to a variety of ideas to counter the narrowmindedness generated in many of our universities today. The next great generation will fight hard for school choice to save our decimated inner cities and, ultimately, the nation itself.

UNBRIDLED OPTIMISM

In looking ahead, I have so far advocated for taking in information from a broader perspective to guard against narrowmindedness, reading books, knowing history, and changing the nation's school system. The order of action is not exactly an easy assignment. So why am I so upbeat concerning the younger generations' potential to change the tide and build for a better future? There are several reasons.

I stated in the introduction that when people discover the truth the hard way, or they were possibly even lied to, it changes them. We currently see the repercussions of 50 years of bad ideas playing out before our eyes in cities and states across our nation. Good ideas have good consequences, and bad ideas have bad consequences. If recent events have not startled you yet, they soon will. For quite some time, our country was like a frog in warm water. The changes were slow initially, and it was difficult to anticipate future effects. Just like the frog who does not do anything as the temperature gradually rises, many citizens in our country did not do anything because things around them did not change much immediately.

The Boomers, as a whole, were caught in the warm water.

The title of the book may suggest that I have a dim view of the Boomers. This is actually not true, and I did use the caveat of "probably" in the title. Nothing is guaranteed. There are great individuals in every generation, and we are all in this together. We can all agree we want the future generations to overcome the adversities we are now encountering. We have finally entered the "hot" phase, but unlike the frog who boils to death, our young are energetic and smart and can change things from the ground up. We are all free to vote for candidates who will contribute to our success in life. The power of the vote has fantastic potential to change the direction of our nation.

Lasting, meaningful change not only comes from the ground up but also from the top down. Good leadership is critical. Most of the good qualities of leaders fall into the three categories of character, vision, and passion. A large portion of this book deals with character. What about vision? Vision, to a great extent, points to purpose, and a person's purpose is also easily derived from the pages of this book. Never forget, purpose drives passion.[11] This book then, and others like it, speak to character, vision, and passion and lay a foundation for good leadership. Your leadership plays out not only in your community and beyond, but also among your circle of friends and your family. You can change things. You have tremendous power to communicate the truth through various social media platforms. Millennials and Xers are uniquely positioned at present to start inserting themselves into leadership situations that will build to even more influence later, ultimately transforming our nation for the better.

I have also volunteered with the younger generations doing hurricane relief in New Orleans, scraping and painting houses on Indian reservations in Montana, and shingling roofs in West Virginia for people who cannot afford to take care of their own homes. The ones I have seen are hard workers, and volunteerism is in their blood. Many have done far more than I ever did at their age, and I believe they will continue. There are never any television crews documenting the thousands and thousands of mundane yet profound acts of kindness that happen every day in our nation. These are the actions that have a tremendous impact on our country.

These are all the reasons I look forward to a magnificent generation rising and turning the tide, overcoming false and destructive ideas with the true and the good.

"Remember those who led you, who spoke the Word of God to you, and considering the result of their conduct, imitate their faith." Hebrews 13:7

RECOMMENDED READING AND RESOURCES

CHRISTIANITY AND LIFE

Mere Christianity, C.S. Lewis, (New York: Macmillan Publishing, 1952).

More Than a Carpenter, Josh McDowell, (Tyndale House Publishers, 1977).

The Purpose Driven Life, Rick Warren, (Grand Rapids: Zondervan, 2002).

Wild at Heart, John Eldredge, (Nashville: Thomas Nelson, 2001).

HISTORY (AND HISTORY OF PHILOSOPHY)

The Closing of the American Mind, Alan Bloom, (New York: Simon & Schuster, 1987).

How Should We Then Live, Francis Schaeffer, (Wheaton, IL: Crossway, 2005).

I Don't Have Enough Faith to Be an Atheist, Norman Geisler and Frank Turek, (Wheaton, Ill.: Crossway books, 2004).

The Triumph of Christianity, Rodney Stark, (New York: HarperCollins, 2011).

INVESTING

The Little Book of Common Sense Investing, John Bogle, (Hoboken, NJ: Wiley and Sons, 2007).

MARRIAGE AND RELATIONSHIPS

The Meaning of Marriage, Timothy Keller, (New York: Penguin Books, 2011).
Real Love, Greg Baer, (New York: Random House, 2003).

SCIENCE

The Creator and the Cosmos, Hugh Ross, (Covina, CA: RTB Press, 2018).
Darwin Devolves, Michael Behe, (New York: HarperCollins, 2019).
Heretic, Matti Leisola, (Seattle: Discovery Institute Press, 2018).

OUR WEBSITE

www.MagGenBook.com to exchange ideas that change lives and build stronger communities.

NOTES

Introduction

1. Mortimer Adler and Charles Van Doren, *How to Read a Book*, (New York: Simon & Schuster,1972), p. 20. This classic book is often mentioned by numerous authors over the last 30 years. The four levels of reading are inspectional, elementary, analytical (underlining, notes in the margin, thorough analysis), and syntopical. Syntopical reading is the highest form of reading and involves a comparative analysis of multiple books that yields conclusions possibly not found in any of the books.

2. Allyson Chiu, "He Is right on all counts: Obama finds rare bipartisan support by bashing woke shaming," The Washington Post, October 31, 2019. https://www.washingtonpost.com/nation/2019/10/31/obama-woke-shaming-bipartisan-support-yang-coulter-gabbard/.

Chapter 1

1. *The American Heritage Dictionary of the English Language*, https://ahdictionary.com/word/search.html?q=success.

2. Richard Ryan and Edward Deci, *Self-Determination Theory: Basic Psychological Needs In Motivation, Development, and Wellness*, (New York:The Guilford Press, 2017), p. 82-86. "SDT (Self-Determination Theory) forwards the proposition that there are specifiable psychological

and social nutrients which, when satisfied within the interpersonal and cultural contexts of an individual's development, facilitate growth, integrity, and well-being. Conversely, when the psychological need satisfactions are frustrated or thwarted, there are serious psychological harms. We refer to these necessary satisfactions for personality and cognitive growth as basic psychological needs...We theorize that, when any of these three basic psychological needs is frustrated or neglected either in a given domain or in general, the individual will show motivational, cognitive, affective, and other psychological decrements of a specifiable nature, such as lowered vitality, loss of volition, greater fragmentation, and diminished well-being."

3.   Ibid., p. 86. They use the term relatedness instead of love and acceptance. "*Relatedness* refers to both experiencing others as responsive and sensitive in being able to be responsive and sensitive to them – that is, feeling connected and involved with others and having a sense of belonging... Relatedness is experienced both in being cared about and in caring. The need is satisfied when others show concern for the individual, as well as when the individual has opportunities to be benevolent toward others, as both directions of caring enhance a sense of connectedness..."

4.   Ibid., p. 86. "*Competence* refers to feeling effective in one's interactions with the social environment – that is, experiencing opportunities and supports for the exercise, expansion, and expression of one's capacities and talents... Where individuals are prevented from developing skills, understanding, or mastery, the competence need will be unmet." Besides relatedness and competence, they include the need of autonomy. Their definition of autonomy somewhat resembles purpose (i.e., people who have no control over their life have difficulty pursuing purpose). "The need for autonomy describes the need of individuals to experience self endorsement and ownership of their actions – to be self regulating in the

technical sense of that term." They go on to say on page 87 that there are many different ways to define and categorize the psychological needs. "Of course, one could take these three general needs and subdivide them, or define the same needs slightly differently, and indeed some such differentiations will follow. Basic psychological needs are, after all, psychological constructs – descriptions of broad categories of satisfactions and frustrations that have been identified with motivational and wellness outcomes. The constructed nature of need variables is illustrated by the fact that different thoughtful approaches to the problem of needs can yield different conceptions."

5. David Seamands, *Healing for Damaged Emotions*, (Colorado Springs: Chariot Victor, 1991), p. 60. Instead of calling them psychological needs, he lists Dr. Maurice Wagner's three essential components of a healthy self-image. The three components are a sense of belongingness (of being loved), a sense of worth and value, and a sense of being competent.

6. Steve Taylor Ph.D., "The Power of Purpose," Psychology Today, July 21, 2013, https://www.psychologytoday.com/us/blog/out-the-darkness/201307/the-power-purpose. He states, "The need for purpose is one of the defining characteristics of human beings. Human beings crave purpose and suffer serious psychological difficulties when we don't have it. Purpose is a fundamental component of human life." He goes on to quote Victor Frankel's famous book, *Man's Search for Meaning*, about Frankel's experiences in World War II concentration camps. Frankel discovered over time that those most likely to survive had a goal or purpose to live.

7. Ron Chernow, *Titan: the life of John D Rockefeller, Sr.*, (New York: Random House, Inc., 1998), p. 101.

8. Russ Crosson, *A Life Well Spent*, (Nashville: Thomas Nelson, 1994), p. 17.

Chapter 2

1.   C.S. Lewis, *Mere Christianity*, (New York: Macmillan Publishing, 1952), p. 97.

2.   Timothy Keller, *The Meaning of Marriage*, (New York: Penguin Books, 2011), p. 77. I have read numerous books on marriage and this is by far the best overall for today's culture. Either the man or the woman can say they do not need a piece of paper to say I love you. However, I think it is far more common for the man to shy away from the initial marriage and long-term commitment it requires.

3.   Michael Rosenfield and Katharina Roesler, "Cohabitation Experience and Cohabitation's Association with Marital Dissolution," Journal of Marriage and Family, September 24, 2018.

4.   Nikki Graf, "Key findings on marriage and cohabitation in the U.S.," The Pew Research Center, November 6, 2019, https://www.pewresearch.org/fact-tank/2019/11/06/key-findings-on-marriage-and-cohabitation-in-the-u-s/

5.   "Marriage and divorce," The American Psychological Association, https://www.apa.org/topics/divorce. The reason they list the divorce rate for the United States between 40% and 50%, and not with greater accuracy, is because there are so many different variables researchers use in calculating the rate. They do note that divorce rates for subsequent marriages are even higher.

6.   "A happy marriage is the union of two good forgivers." Ruth Bell Graham.

7.   John and Stacy Eldridge, *Love and War*, (Colorado Springs: WaterBrook Press, 2009), p. 12. The book is also one of the best overall books ever written on marriage.

8.   Ibid., p. 14.

9.   David Clarke, *I Don't Want a Divorce*, (Grand Rapids, MI: Revell, 2009), p.92-101. His conflict resolution guidance is incredibly discerning.

10. Jordan Peterson, *12 Rules for Life*, (Toronto: Random House Canada, 2018), p. 113- 144. All parents should carefully read this chapter.

11. Keller, *The Meaning of Marriage*, p. 23.

12. Ibid., p. 24-26.

13. Mark Banschick, "The High Failure Rate of Second and Third Marriages," Psychology Today, February 6, 2012, https://www.psychologytoday.com/us/blog/the-intelligent-divorce/201202/the-high-failure-rate-second-and-third-marriages

14. Keller, *The Meaning of Marriage.*, p.113, 114. Keller has a lot to say about friendship in the book and in this section he quotes C.S. Lewis's *The Four Loves*.

15. Greg Baer, *Real Love*, (New York: Random House, 2003), p. 3-15. The author reveals more practical advice on relationships than any single book I have read. The information, more than likely, is new to most readers.

16. Ibid., p. 24.

17. Ibid., p.28- 29.

18. Ibid., p. 48.

19. Ibid., p. 53-54.

Chapter 3

1. Bill Hardekopf, "Do People Really Spend More with Credit Cards?" *Forbes*, July 16, 2018, https://www.forbes.com/sites/billhardekopf/2018/07/16/do-people-really-spend-more-with-credit-cards/#202e460f1c19. "A number of studies have indicated that people do spend more when paying with a credit card. In 2001, Drazen Prelec and Duncan Simester of MIT published the results of their research in Marketing Letters. They found shoppers spend up to 100% more when using their credit card to pay instead of cash."

2. Lyle Daly, "Average Credit Card Processing Fees and Costs in 2020," The Ascent, Research, July 8, 2020. https://www.fool.com/the-ascent/research/average-credit-card-processing-fees-costs-america/.

3. Walter Mischel, *The Marshmallow Test: Why Self-Control Is the Engine of Success*, (New York: Little, Brown and Company,2014), p. 4-6.

4. Melissa Healy, "The surprising thing the marshmallow test reveals about kids in an instant-gratification world," The Los Angeles Times, June 26, 2018, https://www.latimes.com/science/sciencenow/la-sci-sn-marshmallow-test-kids-20180626-story.html. By the time University of Minnesota psychologist Stephanie M. Carlson and colleagues at the University of Washington in Seattle ran the exact same experiment with 540 kids from 2002 to 2012, the changes appeared to be real. Close to 60% of the children tested held out the full 10 minutes for a bigger reward. And only about 12% claimed their reward in the first half-minute. The findings "do make me hopeful," she said. Not only have qualities like perseverance and self-control *not* disappeared; a simple and unchanged measure of those qualities—the marshmallow test—has withstood many trials, including the test of time. "Delay of gratification is still a good bellwether of these self-regulation and executive function skills, and we're learning more every day about how important they are for school readiness and achievement," Carlson said.

5. Robert Kyosaki, *Rich Dad, Poor Dad*, (New York: Warner Books, 2000), p. 61-78. Kyosaki's financial advice is as true now as it was then.

6. Dave Ramsey, *The Total Money Makeover*, (Nashville: Thomas Nelson, 2007. p. 94. An economist or financial advisor may give different advice as to which debt to pay off first. Dave Ramsey's plan, though, works for real people in the real world and has a proven track record of success.

7. Dailycalculators.com, dailycalculators.com/compound-interest-calculator. This is the simplest and best I have found.

8. John Bogle, *The Little Book of Common Sense Investing*, (Hoboken, NJ: Wiley and Sons, 2007), p. 10.

9. J. B. Maverick, "What Is the Average Annual Return for the S&P 500?", Investopedia, February 19, 2020, https://www.investopedia.com/ask/answers/042415/what-average-annual-return-sp-500.asp.

10. John Bogle, *The Little Book of Common Sense Investing*, p.59. Bogle quotes Charles Schwab, "It's fun to play around...it's human nature to try to select the right horse...(But) for the average person, I'm more of an indexer... The predictability is so high...For 10, 15, 20 years you'll be in the 85th percentile of performance. Why would you screw it up?"

Chapter 4

1. Collins online dictionary, https://www.collinsdictionary.com/dictionary/english/tolerance. "Tolerance is the quality of allowing other people to say and do as they like, even if you do not agree or approve of it."

2. Merriam-Webster online dictionary, https://www.merriam-webster.com/dictionary/bigotry. "Bigotry is the obstinate or *intolerant* devotion to one's own *opinions* or prejudices." Bigots, then, are intolerant and do not allow the opinions of others.

3. Andrée Seu Peterson, "All Joking Aside," *World Magazine*, April 11, 2019. The joke is adapted from her shortened version of Soviet jokes.

4. Harold Paget, *Bradford's History of the Plymouth Settlement 1608 – 1650*, p. 115, Printed 1988, published by American Heritage Ministries.

5. Michael Meyer, "The Quiet Revolt That Saved China," *Wall Street Journal*, April 16, 2019.

6. Bernie Sanders – Official Campaign Website, BernieSanders.com, March 18, 2020.

7. Friedrich Hayek, *The Road to Serfdom*, (London: The University Of Chicago Press, 2007), p. 127. "Since under modern conditions we are almost everything dependent on means which our fellow men provide, economic planning would involve direction of the almost whole of our life. There is hardly an aspect of it, from our primary needs to our relations with family and friends, from the nature of our work to the use of our leisure, over which the planner would not exercise his 'conscious control…' Our freedom of choice in a competitive society rests on the fact that, if one person refuses to satisfy our wishes, we can turn to another. But if we face a monopolist we are at his mercy. And an authority directing the whole economic system is the most powerful monopolist conceivable." Chapter 7 is titled Economic Control and Totalitarianism. The entire chapter details how you are not free unless you have some economic freedom to spend money as you need or desire. The book is considered a classic and just as the title suggests, shows how socialism leads to slavery (serfdom).

8. Bret Stephens, "Yes, Venezuela Is A Socialist Catastrophe," *The New York Times,* Jan. 25, 2019, https://www.nytimes.com/2019/01/25/opinion/venezuela-maduro-socialism-government.html.

9. Robert Valencia, "Venezuelans Are Losing A Lot of Weight Amid the Money Crisis," *Newsweek*, Feb 22, 2018, https://www.newsweek.com/venezuelans-are-losing-lot-weight-amid-money-crisis-816886.

10. Marvin Olasky, "Groundhog Years in Argentina," *World Magazine*, Jan. 16, 2020.

11. John Hart, *The Wizard of Id.* 2012, https://sanctification.wordpress.com/2008/11/12/obamas-plans-refuted-in-wizard-of-id-cartoon/.

12. Thomas Ginsburg, Zachary Elkins, and James Melton, "The Lifespan of Written Constitutions," The University Of Chicago Law School, October 15, 2009.

13. Allan Bloom, *The Closing of the American Mind*, (New York: Simon & Schuster, 1987), p. 119.

Chapter 5

1. Allan Bloom, *The Closing of the American Mind*, (New York: Simon & Schuster, 1987), p. 25. He goes on to state that the relativity of truth is not a theoretical insight but a moral postulate to the students entering the University at that time.

2. Ravi Zacharias, *The Grand Weaver*, (Grand Rapids: Zondervan, 2007), p. 106.

3. Norman Geisler and Frank Turek, *I Don't Have Enough Faith to Be an Atheist*, (Wheaton, Ill.: Crossway Books, 2004), p. 56.

4. Ibid., p. 35. Our lists are slightly different but make the exact same point.

5. Jordan Peterson, *12 Rules for Life*, (Toronto: Random House Canada, 2018), p. 230.

6. Geisler and Turek, *I Don't Have Enough Faith to Be an Atheist*, p. 36-38. The acronym ADVENT is adapted from their material defining the characteristics of truth.

7. C.S.Lewis, "Learning in War-Time," *The Weight of Glory*, (New York: HarperCollins Publishers, 2001), p. 58.

8. Geisler and Turek, *I Don't Have Enough Faith to Be an Atheist*, p. 67.

9. Ravi Zacharias, *The End of Reason*, (Grand Rapids: Zondervan, 2008), p. 54.

10. Vishal Mangawaldi, *The Book That Made Your World*, (Nashville: Thomas Nelson, 2011), p. 4.

11. Sally C. Curtin, M.A., and Melonie Heron, PhD, "Death Rates Due To Suicide and Homicide Among Persons Aged 10–24: United States, 2007 – 2017", NCHS Data Brief, No. 352, October, 2017.

12. Jordan Peterson, *12 Rules for Life*, p. 306.

13. Stanley Kurtz, *The Lost History of Western Civilization*, National Association of Scholars, 2020. The report shows in detail where our universities' hatred for Western civilization originated. In the introduction, he states, "Today's radical student activism is rooted in powerful

intellectual currents injected into university life several decades ago. Those currents in the American Academy were skeptical, relativist, historicist, and even nihilist in character."

14. Geisler and Turek, *I Don't Have Enough Faith to Be an Atheist*, p. 67.

15. Haim G. Ginott, *Teacher and Child: A Book for Parents and Teachers*, (New York: Avon books, 1975).

Chapter 6

1. Mitch Leslie, "There are millions of protein factories in every cell. Surprise, they are not all the same," The American Association for the Advancement of Science, June 21, 2017.

2. Elizabeth Pennisi, "Human Genome Is Much More Than Just Genes," Science Magazine, September 5, 2012, https://www.sciencemag.org/news/2012/09/human-genome-much-more-just-genes#.

3. Ann Condon, et al., "Will Biologists Become Computer Scientists?" EMBO reports, September 19, 2018, as reported in the NCBI (National Center for Biotechnology Information), https://www.ncbi.nlm.nih.gov/pmc/articles/PMC6123653/. "Like computers, living cells are synthesized by algorithmic machines based on a construction scheme."

4. Bill Gates, *The Road Ahead*, (Viking, Penguin Group,1996, Revised Edition), p. 228.

5. Francis Collins, *The Language of God*, (New York: Simon & Schuster, 2006), p. 123-124. Dr. Collins led the government side of mapping out the human genome. He believes in theistic, guided evolution.

6. Walter Isaacson, *Einstein: His Life and Universe*, (New York: Simon & Schuster, 2007), p. 254. "According to his field equations, a static universe was impossible because the gravitational forces would pull all the

matter together. This did not accord with what most astronomers thought they had observed. As far as they knew, the universe consisted only of our Milky Way galaxy, and it all seemed pretty stable and static...To keep the matter in the universe from imploding, Einstein added a 'repulsive force': a little addition to his general relativity equations to counterbalance gravity in the overall scheme."

7.   Ibid., p. 255.

8.   Hugh Ross, *The Creator and the Cosmos*, (Covina, CA:RTB Press, 2018), p. 115. Dr. Ross earned a PhD in astronomy from the University of Toronto. For years he did research on quasars and galaxies as a postdoctoral fellow at the California Institute of technology. Appendix A of his book is a great summary for the evidence for the fine-tuning of the universe. Appendix B is also an excellent source for listing the fine-tuning of the Milky Way galaxy, solar system, and the earth.

9.   Walter Isaacson, *Einstein: His Life and Universe*, p. 335.

10.   Geraint Lewis and Luke Barnes, *A Fortunate Universe*, (Cambridge: Cambridge University Press, 2016), p. 353. The authors state on page 241 and 242, "Luke (Dr. Barnes) has published a review of the scientific literature on fine-tuning, carefully summarizing the conclusions of over 200 published papers in the field. These papers have built on the original work of key physicists, Carter, Silk, Carr, Reese, Davies, Barrow and Tipler, who pioneered the field. Their calculations have been refined using cutting edge models and methods. Sometimes, new options for life have opened up, and sometimes life has turned out to be more fine-tuned than previously thought. On balance, the fine-tuning of the universe for life has stood up well under the scrutiny of physicists... This reaction (opposition to fine-tuning arguments) might stem from the belief that fine-tuning is the invention of a bunch of religious believers who hijack physics to their own ends. This is not the case: the field began in physics journals and remains with

physicists such as Barrow, Carr, Carter, Davies, Deutsch, Ellis, Green, Guth, Harrison, Hawking, Linde, Page, Penrose, Polkinghorne, Rees, Sandage, Smolin, Susskind, Tegmark, Tipler, Vilenkin, Weinberg, Wheeler and Wilczek.

11. Ibid., p. 141.

12. Hugh Ross, *The Creator and the Cosmos*, p. 54.

13. Geraint Lewis and Luke Barnes, *A Fortunate Universe*, (Cambridge: Cambridge University Press, 2016), p. 76. Throughout the book, Dr. Lewis and Dr. Barnes show what happens to the universe when you change the known properties of physics. Just like moving extremely sensitive dials on a control instrument, changing the parameters in the universe results in either nothing or chaos.

14. Ibid., p. 63.

15. David Waltham, *Lucky Planet*, (New York: Basic Books, 2014), p. 43, 44. The author, an astrobiologist and geophysicist, describes on page 37 and 38 the 12 parameters that greatly influence life on earth. They are metal mass, rock mass, volatile mass, gas mass, illumination, internal heat, location in the galaxy, lifetime of a star, earth's rate of rotation, the circularity of its orbit, the angle between a planet's axis and its orbit, and locations of other planets in the system.

16. Hugh Ross, *The Creator and the Cosmos*, p. 220.

17. Graphene, University of Manchester, https://www.graphene.manchester.ac.uk/learn/applications/.

18. Robert F. Service, "Electricity Turns Garbage into Graphene," *Science Magazine*, June 27, 2020, https://www.sciencemag.org/news/2020/01/electricity-turns-garbage-graphene.

19. Andrew Montford and Mikko Paunio, "WMO Secretary-General Rejects Climate Doomsters and Extremists," Global Warming Policy Forum, June 9, 2019. Petteri Taalas, speaking to Finland's financial newspaper Talouselämä ("The Journal"), on 6 September 2019. https://www.thegwpf.com/wmo-boss-says-climate-discussion-has-gone-off-the-rails/.

Chapter 7

1. Francis Schaeffer, *How Shall We Then Live* (Wheaton, IL: Crossway, 2005), p. 19, 20.

2. Douglas Axe, *Undeniable: How Biology Confirms Our Intuition That Life Is Designed*, (New York: HarperCollins, 2016), p.57.

3. Mattie Liesola and Jonathan Witt, *Heretic: One Scientists Journey From Darwin to Design*, (Seattle: Discovery Institute Press, 2018), p. 36-37. The quote was taken from "The Origin of Life: an inside Story – 2016 Lectures," by James Tour.

4. Michael Behe, *Darwin's Black Box*, (New York: Free Press, 1996), p. 42-45. Dr. Behe fully covers the example of irreducible complexity and the mousetrap in these pages.

5. Ibid., p. 69-71.

6. Rick Lewis, "Flew's Change-of-mind About God," Philosophy Now, Issue 79, June/July 2010, https://philosophynow.org/issues/79/Flews_change-of-mind_about_God.

7. Michael Behe, *The Edge of the Evolution*, (New York: Free Press, 2007), p. 194.

8. Ibid., p. 146. On page 126 the author states, "... Not only do the shapes of two proteins have to match, but the chemical properties of their surfaces must be complementary as well, to attract each other. If the shapes of two protein surfaces match each other but their chemical properties don't, the two surfaces won't stick; they might bump together in the cell, but if so they would quickly drift apart." The book details how finicky proteins are in regards to their shape fitting into the shape of other proteins.

9. Stephen Meyer, *Signature in the Cell*, (New York: HarperCollins, 2009), p. 15. In this great book, Dr. Meyer demonstrates how unique information is. The genetic code represents complex and specified information. The code is complex, but it is also specified since the exact arrangement builds micro-machines. Specified information is specified either by

pattern or function. An example of pattern would be Mount Rushmore showing the faces of four presidents. An example of specified function would be a computer program that runs an automated assembly line. This is exactly what DNA does.

10. Ibid., p. 17.

11. Ibid., p. 347.

12. Thomas Nagel, *Mind and Cosmos: Why the Materialist Neo-Darwinian Conception of Nature Is Almost Certainly False*, (New York: Oxford University Press, 2012), p. 6.

13. Ibid., 128.

14. Stephen Meyer, *Darwin's Doubt*, (New York: HarperCollins, 2013), p. 137.

15. Ibid., p. 13.

16. Ibid., p. 72.

17. Ibid., p. 262.

18. Jonathan Wells, *Icons of Evolution*, (Washington DC: Regenery Publishing, 2000), p.221. Dr. Wells earned his second PhD at Berkeley in molecular and cellular biology. He has updated much of his research in *Zombie Science: More Icons of Evolution*, 2017.

19. Ibid., p. 91.

20. Ibid., p. 156.

21. Ibid., p. 174-175.

22. Douglas Axe, *Undeniable: How Biology Confirms Our Intuition That Life Is Designed*, p. 81-82.

23. Ibid., p. 96-97.

24. Michael Behe, *Darwin Devolves*, (New York: HarperCollins, 2019), p. 201.

25. Ibid., p. 256.

26. Scientific Dissent from Darwinism, https://dissentfromdarwin.org/about/. "The list is growing and includes scientists from the US National Academy of Sciences, Russian, Hungarian and Czech National

Academies, as well as from universities such as Yale, Princeton, Stanford, MIT, UC Berkeley, UCLA, and others."

27. David Gelernter, "Giving Up Darwin: A Fond Farewell to a Brilliant and Beautiful Theory," Claremont Review of Books, Spring 2019. http://www.theinternationalchronicles.com/2019/12/29/giving-up-darwin-a-fond-farewell-to-a-brilliant-and-beautiful-theory/.

28. Science Daily, "Stunning Details of Brain Connections Revealed," November 17, 2010, https://www.sciencedaily.com/releases/2010/11/101117121803.htm. "Researchers at the Stanford University School of Medicine, applying a state-of-the-art imaging system to brain-tissue samples from mice, have been able to quickly and accurately locate and count the myriad connections between nerve cells in unprecedented detail, as well as to capture and catalog those connections' surprising variety."

29. Encyclopaedia Britannica, Big-Bang Model, Cosmology, https://www.britannica.com/science/big-bang-model.

30. Geraint Lewis and Luke Barnes, *A Fortunate Universe*, (Cambridge: Cambridge University Press, 2016), p. 147.

31. Hugh Ross, *The Creator and the Cosmos*, (Covina, CA:RTB Press, 2018), p. 220.

32. John Horgan, "Remembering Big Bang Basher Fred Hoyle," Scientific American, April 7, 2020. https://blogs.scientificamerican.com/cross-check/remembering-big-bang-basher-fred-hoyle/.

33. Geraint Lewis and Luke Barnes, *A Fortunate Universe*, p. 165.

34. Hugh Ross, *The Creator and the Cosmos*, p. 21.

35. James Anderson, *What's Your Worldview*, (Wheaton: Crossway, 2014), p. 89-90.

36. Dinesh D'Souza, *What's so Great about Christianity*, (Washington DC: Regnery Publishing, 2007), p. 123-124.

37. Francis Collins, *The Language of God*, (New York: Simon & Schuster, 2006), p. 152.

38. Peter W. Stoner, and Robert C. Newman, *Science Speaks*, (Chicago: Moody Press, 1976), p. 106-112.

39. Norman Geisler and Frank Turek, *I Don't Have Enough Faith to Be an Atheist*, (Wheaton, Ill.: Crossway Books, 2004), p. 225.

40. Ibid., p. 20.

Chapter 8

1. David Platt, *Radical*, (Colorado Springs: Multnomah, 2010), p. 33.

2. Francis Schaeffer, *How Shall We Then Live* (Wheaton, IL: Crossway, 2005), p. 151, 132.

3. Rodney Stark, *The Triumph of Christianity* (New York: HarperCollins, 2011), p. 281.

4. Vishal Mangawaldi, *The Book That Made Your World* (Nashville: Thomas Nelson, 2011), p. 194.

5. Ibid, p. 72.

6. Ibid. p. 36.

7. Rodney Stark, *The Triumph of Christianity* (New York: HarperCollins, 2011), p. 217.

8. Ibid. p. 337.

9. Paul Chamberlain, *Why People Stop Believing* (Eugene, Ore.: Cascade Books, 2018), p. 38.

10. Ravi Zacharias, *The End of Reason*, (Grand Rapids: Zondervan, 2008), p. 66, 67.

11. C.S. Lewis, *Mere Christianity* (New York: Macmillan, 1952), p. 45.

12. Tim Keller, *Making Sense of God* (New York: Penguin Random House, 2016), p. 39, 40.

13. Norman Geisler and Frank Turek, *I Don't Have Enough Faith to Be an Atheist* (Wheaton, Ill.: Crossway books, 2004), p. 225.

14. J. Warner Wallace, *Cold- Case Christianity* (Colorado Springs: David C. Cook, 2013), p. 108.

15. Norman Geisler and Frank Turek, *I Don't Have Enough Faith to Be an Atheist*, p. 229.

16. Timothy Paul Jones, *Misquoting Truth*, (Downers Grove, Il: InterVarsity Press, 2007), p. 47.

17. Josh D. McDowell, *The New Evidence That Demands a Verdict* (copyright © 1999 by Josh D. McDowell), XXV.

18. Lee Strobel, *The Case for Christ* (Grand Rapids: Zondervan, 2016), p. 21.

19. C. S. Lewis, *Mere Christianity* (New York: Macmillan, 1952), p. 45, 46.

20. Paul Chamberlain, *Why People Stop Believing* (Eugene, Ore.: Cascade Books, 2018), p.177.

21. C. S. Lewis, *Miracles* (New York: Macmillan, 1960), p. 61, 95.

22. Paul Chamberlain, *Why People Stop Believing* (Eugene, Ore.: Cascade Books, 2018), p. 135.

23. Francis Schaeffer, *How Should We Then Live* (Wheaton, IL: Crossway, 2005), p.151, 152.

24. Allan Bloom, *The Closing of the American Mind* (New York: Simon & Schuster, 1987), p.143.

25. Timothy Keller, *The Reason for God*, (New York: Penguin Books, 2008), p. 40.

Chapter 9

1. Norman Geisler and Frank Turek, *I Don't Have Enough Faith to Be an Atheist* (Wheaton, Ill.: Crossway books, 2004), p. 51. Geisler and Turek

quote James Sire's seminar called *Why Should Anyone Believe Anything at All?* The four reasons people believe what they believe are sociological, psychological, religious, and philosophical.

2. David Plotnikoff, "Zinn's influential history textbook has problems, says Stanford education expert," Stanford News, December 20, 2012, https://news.stanford.edu/news/2012/december/wineburg-historiography-zinn-122012.html.

3. Sam Wineburg, *Why Learn History (When It's Already on Your Phone)*, (Chicago: University of Chicago press, 2018), p. 56. Every thinking person should read all of chapter 3, titled Committing Zinns.

4. Ibid., p. 59-60.

5. Ibid., p. 61-70.

6. Josh McDowell, *More Than a Carpenter* (Tyndale House Publishers, 1977), p. 49-50.

7. Armstrong Williams, "Baltimore's failing schools are a tragedy of criminal proportions," *The Hill*, September 13, 2017.

8. Thomas Sowell, *Charter Schools and Their Enemies*, (New York: Basic Books, 2020), p. 56. The author compares traditional schools with charter schools. The schools compared had to have a similar ethnic composition of students, taught in the very same building, and had to have one or more classes at the same grade level in the same building. New York City had the most schools that met the criteria. The charter schools outperformed traditional schools by large margins. The margins are so glaring that traditional school systems are trying to prevent charter schools by not allowing buildings. Traditional schools are also using political clout to prohibit the spread of charter schools.

9. Center for Research on Education Outcomes © 2015 CREDO, Urban Charter School Study Report on 41 Regions 2015 (Stanford University, Stanford, CA), v-vi, https://credo.stanford.edu.

10. Larry Schweikart, *What Would the Founders Say?* (New York: Penguin Group, 2011), p. 29.

11. Rick Warren, *The Purpose Driven Life*, (Grand Rapids: Zondervan, 2002), p. 33. The book has sold 50 million copies and is printed in 85 languages, so the author must have gotten something right.

ACKNOWLEDGMENTS

We thank our families for putting up with us during this project. I also am grateful for my wife who encouraged me tremendously and helped with the difficult editing process. We greatly appreciate the technical review or help we received from Steve Barnes, Steve Blevins, Steve Busskohl, and Mike Server. I am always thankful for Alan, Bill, and Todd and our weekly guy's time where we talk about all things essential and otherwise.

INDEX